The Achievers

THE ACHIEVERS

Six Styles of Personality and Leadership

GERALD D. BELL

Preston-Hill, Inc.
Chapel Hill, North Carolina

To my parents, Florence and Louis, and my family,
Tina, Kathryn, and Sharon, whose enriching sensitivity
to the achievement potential in their lives made this
book possible for me.

Contents

I have found the ideas presented in this book to be very helpful to me personally, and I hope they will help you to find greater personal satisfaction in your life and increased effectiveness in relating to others. The key to this goal is self-awareness. Most people readily understand effectiveness, but few comprehend personal satisfaction, or what I call psychological health.

Who is the most psychologically healthy individual you know personally? What is he or she like? A psychologically healthy person—an achiever—is one who feels genuinely happy with himself; he has inner peace. He feels good about who he is, where he came from, and where he is going in life. He feels safe, accepted and loved by others. His self-awareness is heightened by his inner knowledge of his weaknesses and strengths. He accepts them without guilt or shame, but with a positive feeling that: "I'm okay." His high self-esteem allows him to accept his successes and failures in a natural manner. In addition, he is able to give love, affection, and care to others genuinely and warmly without being neurotically dependent or domineering. He is real and spontaneous; he moves toward people for he is willing to express his feelings.

A psychologically healthy person is exhilarated with his life and is motivated to make himself more fulfilled, genuine, and effective. He is seldom overly tense; he sleeps peacefully and relaxation comes naturally for him. He is in a continual process of being, living, and becoming what he is able to become—self-actualized. He lets his life unfold along the paths of his unique abilities, interests, and needs, for he becomes what his potentials will allow. Living for him is the process of fulfilling what is inside him, not what others expect or demand of him. He is contented, involved, and active in pursuing those things that interest him. Typically, his pursuits contribute meaningfully to others. He is, in short, an achiever, an actualizer.

By no means is he perfect; there is no such human being. Anger, frustration, stubborness, pride, nervousness, depression, fear, rejection, and loneliness all cross his doorstep. However, they usually stem from genuine problems in the situations in which he is involved rather than from his own personal weakness, and last only a short time.

The achiever, then, is a person who is confident, warm, spontaneous, creative, realistic, compassionate, and effective. Do you know someone like this? Do you wonder why he (she) seems so contented, well-rounded, and harmonious in his (her) relationships, while yours might be sporadic and sometimes downright miserable?

This book is designed to help you answer these questions and to become an achiever. I choose the term ''achiever'' to indicate the most psychologically healthy person because he is also, in general, the most effective. To be both healthy and effective, in my judgment, is the highest goal a human being can achieve. Many assume an achiever is a compulsive striver. I prefer to label the overly aggressive, status-seeking person a performer, and to retain the positive connotations the term achiever possesses for the more balanced, competence-seeking person. To understand the achiever personality, you need to analyze five additional types—the commander, attacker, avoider, pleaser, and performer. They give you a basis to compare the achiever with. Understanding these six types of personality has helped me achieve greater degrees of fulfillment in my own life and has led others I have worked with to a more enriching professional and private life.

My students, patients, and clients, mostly individuals in active leadership positions, have said that by learning about these six personality types they were more able to clearly (1) understand why they behaved as they did, (2) explain the actions of those with whom they relate closely, (3) select a more proper match between their own personality and careers, (4) choose a properly matching spouse 'or to enrich their marriage), (5) lead others more effectively and (6) become more self-confident. In addition, those who have studied these personality concepts say that they helped in understanding more deeply many personal experiences and formal readings about personality, leadership, and organizational behavior.

When reading about each personality type, do not be disturbed to find signs of all six in yourself. This is much like the medical student who feels he has every disease he is currently studying. It takes careful diagnosis, time, self-confidence, feedback, and much courage to be honest enough to see yourself, but the reward in personal growth and fulfillment is worth it, for the facts are friendly (Carl Rogers, *On Becoming a Person*, p. 25, 1961). The truth is necessary for you to grow.

Personal growth takes your commitment, but your rewards will be self-generating. So try to experience this book rather than just read it. Try to tie it to your own life, take it home with you, work with it, use the ideas. For, as Abraham Maslow suggests, "Self-knowledge seems to be the major path to self-improvement" (Abraham Maslow, *Motivation and Personality* p. 218, 1970). I think there is no better investment than in your own growth toward excellence as a human being (John Gardner, *Excellence*, 1961).

The theories of personality presented here are carefully tested and analyzed concepts derived from my experience and research, much of which is based on intimate counseling, consulting, teaching, training, and psychological analyses of over 3,000 individuals during the past eight years. I have used these ideas quite successfully in these relationships, and now I would like to share them with more people than I can communicate with personally. This is why I have written *The Achievers*.[1]

---

1. A more technical analysis of these data will be presented in forthcoming professional publications. A brief review of the methodology appears in the Appendix. The names used in this book are fictitious, but the cases are real.

Acknowledgments

May I express deep thanks to the following individuals who have helped me greatly: J. Stacy Adams, Richard Calhoon, Thomas Jerdee, Dannie Moffie, Ben Rosen, and George Welsh of the University of North Carolina; Paul Lawrence, Jay Lorsch, Anthony Athos, and Chris Argyris of Harvard University; Elton Jackson of the University of Indiana; Gordon Barker, Blaine Mercer, and Judson Pearson of the University of Colorado; Peter Range of Time, Inc.; all my patients, clients, and students; Jerry Hopper, and especially Dean Maurice W. Lee, who provided support and encouragement. My intellectual debts I owe directly to Carl Rogers, Abraham Maslow, and David McClelland.

I regret that there are many more examples of men than women in *The Achievers*, but at the time this was written, there were so few women in leadership roles. We are making great progress, but we need to make much more and eliminate glass ceilings to provide equality of opportunity and the deepest respect for each individual.

Use of the pronoun "he" is for uniformity only. I wish there were an unbiased pronoun. A female pronoun is an acceptable substitute, with the exception of gender specific instances, such as mother or father.

PART I

CHAPTER 1

Six Styles of Personality and Motivation

Who is the most self-confident person that you know well? Write in his initials. _____Who is the most effective leader you have ever known personally? Write in his initials. _____

What causes the people you have just listed to be so strikingly effective and psychologically healthy? What makes them distinct? What motivates them to act as they do? What basic psychological needs do they seek to satisfy?

Nine out of ten people select as the most effective, healthy individual they know, someone with a great need to achieve. This book is titled *The Achievers*, in fact, because this is the type of personality I feel we should seek and is the one I believe we should attempt to foster in our children and society.

When I began my search for a deeper understanding of personality, at least two basic psychological needs (to achieve and to command) and possibly a third (to avoid or to affiliate) had been briefly described by others.[1] I ended this journey, however, having discovered six major personality needs—to command, to attack, to avoid, to please, to perform, and to achieve.[2] Which of these per-

---

1. The research on the need to avoid failure and to affiliate was confusing and overlapping.

2. Probably there are more, and future research will add to these six types by progressing to finer levels of analysis and specialization. There is, therefore, no finality in six categories. Each need causes us—you and me—to behave in a unique fashion. We can, therefore, label our behavior as a personality type that corresponds with our major psychological needs.

sonality types sounds like it might be you? Are you a commander? Are you an attacker? Are you an avoider? Are you a pleaser? Are you a performer? Or, are you an achiever? What are your motivations? What basic psychological needs do you seek to satisfy? How effective and self-confident are you? You will find answers to these questions if you examine the following picture for a few seconds and then make up a story about what you see in the picture. Who are these people? What do you think is going on? What has just happened? What is going to happen in the future? Use your imagination.

Write your story here

In addition to the story you just wrote, for you to understand your motivations more accurately, you will find it helpful to answer the following questions:

1. Who is the most effective person or best leader you have ever known personally?

2. Please write a short description of him. What are his major characteristics?

3. Who is the worst person or worst leader you have ever known personally?

4. Please write a short description of him.

5. Who is the person that you know well other than your spouse (or closest friend if not married) who you are most naturally attracted to?

6. If you were recovering from a serious illness and were confined to your hospital bed for two more months, who would you select to be in the bed next to you? (It must be someone you know personally. It cannot be a wife or relative. You must rule out sexual motivations.)

Check the appropriate box for each question: A □, very much; B □, much; C □, some; D □, not much; E □, little; F □, very little.

—Compared to Most People—

7) How orderly and domineering are you?   A □ B □ C □ D □ E □ F □
8) How critical and argumentative are you?   A □ B □ C □ D □ E □ F □
9) How shy and quiet are you?   A □ B □ C □ D □ E □ F □
10) How much do you like to please others?   A □ B □ C □ D □ E □ F □
11) How eager for success and recognition are you?   A □ B □ C □ D □ E □ F □
12) How self-confident and self-fulfilled are you?   A □ B □ C □ D □ E □ F □

The answers to these questions appears in the appendix on p. 199.

Psychologists have discovered that you project your personality into situations, especially when they are ambiguous. So, when I ask you to make up a story about the preceding picture, you probably unknowingly transmit your personality needs into your story. You see those things you are interested in—those things that motivate you. You see the picture differently from others because your unique combination of needs causes you to be interested in a particular set of topics. You make up stories that reflect your special needs and motivations. What concerns you is what motivates you. What you think about in your spare time is what you are really concerned with. Your story, consequently, is a small sample from which to gain some insights into your own psychological needs, for it suggests which of the six needs—to command, attack, avoid, please, perform, or achieve—you possess most significantly. (More detail concerning what these "story tests" mean appears in later chapters.) Briefly, your story can be characterized as fitting into one of the following six basic personality types.

The Six Major Individual Psychological Needs

Here, then, are the six personality types in a concise form.

The Need to Command: The Commander The commander needs to control whatever situation he confronts, dominate every group he is in, and live an orderly, systematic life. He dislikes ambiguity and uncertainty. He sees his world in clear-cut categories, and approaches new situations in a dogmatic and stubborn manner. If the story you wrote expresses these ideas, you probably have a high need to command.

One Commander, the tall, muscular director of a national health organization, who walked with precision, talked with clarity, and thought in straight logic, wrote the following story about the same picture you have just described:

> This group of technical specialists will carry out the director's plan to establish a new billing system for their national network of state projects. He is explaining how each district will coordinate their work under his plan. They will report weekly so they can be kept under control. The director, who is sitting in the center of the group,

is going to ensure that his plan works. He has a favorite saying, "If a person doesn't do his job right, chew up a glass and spit it out at him. Cut him up so he follows instructions next time!"

French President Charles De Gaulle demonstrated many commander traits. Similarly, General Patton seemed to be a full-blooded commander.

The Need to Attack: The Attacker The attacker needs to release his hostilities without accepting responsibility or depending on others. He likes to hit others and to run from obligations. He tears down a plan but offers no solutions. Being an authority rebel, he loves to argue and to debate. He is sarcastic, cynical, and negative. If you perceive these ideas in your story, chances are you have many attacker needs.

In describing the previous picture, one attacker, who was a stockbroker with a small, unconventional firm, and who had a spotty career with his customers, wrote:

> These are a bunch of two-fisted executives fooling themselves that they are doing some important work. Really they talk a lot but don't do much. Two of the guys are making fun of the speaker, and the one man looking out the window is thinking that he is wasting his time. The leader is trying to get the group to do what he wants, but they are telling him, "We know what would happen if we did. We'd all get in trouble with top management again. So why don't you sit down and shut up."

Hitler was a clear case of an attacker. He was rebellious, caustic and severe. Fighting was his strength. Viciousness was his cause (Allan Bullock, *Hitler*, 1964).

The Need to Avoid: The Avoider The avoider needs to avoid failure. His goal in life is to hide. He wants to stay out of trouble. He is dependent on others to lead him. He possesses little self-confidence, and he prefers assignments that are stable and routine. He takes few personal risks and sets low goals for himself. If your story outlined these traits it suggests you are an avoider.

One avoider, the quiet, middle-aged husband of a classic commander wife, wrote the following story about the picture:

The man sitting is telling the group about what happened at the last sales convention. He was having cocktails with a client, a young, attractive woman, when some of his friends walked into the nightclub. He tried to explain that he was on business, but he knew they would tell his wife and she would kill him. He doesn't know what to do. If he tells her, and they don't, he gets in trouble for nothing. If he decides not to tell her, and they do, he really suffers. In any case she already is angry at his having spent so much money on the trip.

President Calvin Coolidge was a prime example of an avoider.

The Need to Please: The Pleaser   The pleaser needs to make others like and approve of him. He seeks acceptance from all with whom he associates by being kind and generous and by going along with others, because he would rather make friends than perform a task well. He prefers assignments that involve dealing with people on an easy, sociable basis. These themes in your story characterize you as a pleaser.

One pleaser, the publicity director for a candy manufacturing company, wrote this story about the picture:

> These guys are trying to determine who gets to tee off first in their golf match Sunday. John, the one standing, is kidding the others about who in the group gets to play him. The one smiling is really enjoying this conversation. He is saying to himself, "What a great bunch of guys I work with. We really have a team relationship, except for Edward there who is looking out the window with his back turned to the group." Maybe he is trying to make the others look bad. They try to get him to join in.

The Need to Perform: The Performer   The performer needs to gain prestige and recognition. To do this he maneuvers others and tries to make an impression. He strives diligently to be proper and respectable. Accordingly, he changes his values to go along with the most advantageous positions, and he is very hard to pin down. He seeks those tasks which maximize his image and prestige, regardless of whether he believes in the tasks. If you wrote a story which contains these themes it reflects your performer needs.

A successful twenty-seven-year-old advertising executive wrote this story about the picture:

The man sitting in the center is just finishing selling the group his plan for initiating a new product in the breakfast foods division. He had done his homework. They were impressed. He figured out what each member of the group wanted and integrated his preferences into the plan so that each person would go along with him. Then he got his buddy in the group, the one standing, to make the presentation. He is now closing their teamwork with an enticing pitch about how they will all look like heroes when it works. He has a sly grin on his face. He has talked them into buying his plan. He feels he has won.

This executive was obviously a star performer. Many politicians display these performer qualities—Lyndon Johnson and Huey Long, for example, were shrewd performers.

The Need to Achieve: The Achiever The achiever needs to maximize his potential, to reach his highest levels of competence, to become self-fulfilled. He is problem-centered and goal-oriented rather than self-centered, since he has much self-confidence and self-reliance. He works toward challenging, yet realistic goals. He accepts feedback about his results and likes to explore creative new ways to reach his objectives. He devotes himself to things he believes in, not those that merely give him prestige or money. If you imagined a story filled with these concepts you are likely an achiever.

One achiever, an attractive, thirty-eight-year-old mother of four who eschewed make-up, fancy clothes or other decorative symbols and taught school because she loved it and considered it important to mankind, wrote the following story about the picture:

> These people are formulating a new style of teaching for their school. They have gotten excited for they are going to be able to implement the theories they have been studying for the last year. The kids will grow under this new design, because it stresses individualized teaching and experiential learning. They feel good, because their principal just approved their plan.

Abraham Lincoln, Franklin Roosevelt, and Benjamin Franklin exemplify achievers for the most part. Many great coaches, such as basketball coaches Dean Smith at the University of North Carolina and John Wooden of UCLA, reflect the achiever character.

The Six Psychological Needs in Combination

These six personality needs are pure types—classical personality models. You probably do not fit exactly into one type but are a mixture of these models. The degree to which you have each of these needs varies, however. You are unique, complex, dynamic. Consequently you, like most of us, are difficult to understand. Typically you have within your mixture of needs one of the six pure types as a dominant type, your primary motivation. It is the major determinant of your behavior and is relatively obvious to your friends and yourself. You also have a secondary need, but it influences your behavior less significantly than your dominant need. You may, for instance, be predominately a performer with a secondary need as an achiever. Or, if your dominant need is to avoid, your secondary need is likely to please or to achieve, for example.

Beyond your dominant and secondary needs, you will perhaps have a third need and, of course, each of the others to a lesser degree. But they are usually difficult to perceive. They motivate you only slightly.

Typically, then, when you evaluate another person, you are able to see his two or three predominant needs and no more. You recognize a colleague as an attacker/commander/avoider, for instance. Often in your first attempts to analyze a member of your family or a friend in these six personality types, you will discover that your subject seems to be an equal blend of two or three types. This is natural. After more careful analysis you will be able to designate his dominant need.

You must remember, again, that these six models are ideal types. Most people are combinations of these ideal types. To accurately understand an individual you must measure the degree of each of the six needs he possesses. Your spouse might be, for example, 50 percent pleaser, 30 percent avoider and 20 percent performer. Or, your boss might be 70 percent commander, 20 percent achiever and 10 percent attacker, for instance. What do you think are your own three major needs?

Most Frequently Found Combinations of Needs

Although any combination of the six personality needs is possible, certain types combine more frequently than others to form your dominant and secondary (and other) needs.

The most frequent combinations tend to be personality types next to each other on the Six Factor Personality Diamond. (See Diagram 1.) For example, if your primary need is to perform, it is most likely that your secondary need would either be to achieve or to attack because they are similar to the need to perform. If your secondary need is to achieve, it is likely your third need is to please. This third need, however, will not be very visible and will not

CHART 1

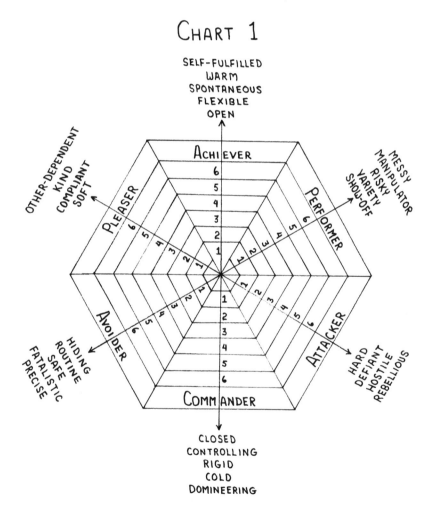

THE SIX-M PERSONALITY DIAMOND

influence your behavior as much as your first two needs do. Nevertheless, a careful observer will be able to distinguish traces of your third need, and if you get into a situation that reinforces pleasing behavior, this need will rise to the surface. Any combination of these needs is possible, but the adjacent needs usually go together.[3]

Each of these six types appear in all walks of life. Ministers, atheists, liberals, conservatives, old, young, well-educated, uneducated, husbands, wives, wealthy, and poor all have these six types within their midst.

Adjacent Needs Combine

Motivations that are most similar are adjacent. Motivations that are opposite are the most incompatible. Pleasers and attackers, for instance, are quite incompatible. Performers and avoiders are mutually frustrating. Achievers contradict commanders' basic needs. In each of these instances, if a person tries to satisfy one of these needs, he directly frustrates the opposite need. When a pleaser, for example, tries to get close to an attacker, the attacker assaults him.

Individuals develop specific personal goals according to their major needs. The numbers from one to six indicate varying degrees of each need. People all exert energy to attain their goals, to satisfy their particular needs, and they all seek to avoid blocks or frustrations of those needs. Similarly, people with each of the six categories seek environments—jobs, people, situations—that are most similar, and thus, compatible. They seek environments where they can reach their *best-fit-adjustments*, where they can act out their needs and be most effective and contented in their best-fit-adjustment situation, and least effective and least satisfied in their *worst-fit-adjustment* or worst-matched-situation. Pleasers seek pleaser environments. Performers search for performer environments, and so forth.

We Were Born to Achieve I have come to the conclusion that when we were born we had a natural urge, a human responsiveness, a biogenetic heritage to be achievers. Infants, before they are taught different needs, tend to react spontaneously according to their feel-

---

3. Typical combinations for example are the performer and commander needs. This produces the famous entrepreneur. The commander pleaser combination produces the paternalistic or benevolent dictator, etc.

ings; to smile and laugh when happy, to cry and express anger and rage when frustrated. Babies for the most part have a natural curiosity, a desire to explore, to search their environments. They listen intently; they express their feelings authentically. In diagram 1, the enlarged center of the achievement diamond depicts this point.

During our first days we begin to receive a wide variety of stimulations. By the time we are two or three years old we have been exposed to some *commander* experiences that thrust upon us rewards for being dominant, orderly, and rigid. Maybe our father was our model for these traits. We have had training to *attack*, to express our hostilities to rebel against authorities. Our oldest sister, for example, might have thrashed and gouged us because of sibling jealousy. This sensitized us to hostility.

We were given many situations which heightened our need to *avoid* being hurt. We might have been severely frightened by some event—being sick, burnt, cut or hit—or warned and worried over by our grandmother. Also, in our early years we were, to some degree, smothered with kindness, love, warm protection—we were rewarded for *pleasing* others.

Our need to *perform* was heightened by the urging we received to air our silly, childlike sayings, funny pronunciations and budding skills in front of our parents, friends and relatives. We were taught the importance of showing off. Similarly, we received encouragement to be ourselves, to say what we felt and we were still accepted by adults because we were "innocent." We were allowed to be authentic, to be *achievers* because we were still "young."

It is almost as if in our early years we are living on a roulette wheel that spins us around past each of these six major types of training environments. As we pass through each training region we get a taste of what it is like. We learn a little of what it means to need to command, avoid, and so forth. Typically, the wheel stops, however, at those areas where our parents' personalities fall.

If your parents are both performers, for instance, this is your number. Your wheel spins little beyond performer training. You become, in a sense, locked into this training environment. Although you have exposure to the other areas, your strings are pulled by performer experiences. You learn to become a young performer. Your natural, human instincts to be an achiever are overridden by the power of the performer situational moldings you receive.

As you leave home you seek out performer situations—friends, hobbies, play, sports, jobs, schools, teachers, college majors and spouses that complement your needs to perform. These complementary performer environments further reinforce your needs to perform and diminish your other five needs. You have entered a performer life spiral.

After you acquire significant training in one or more of these need-producing environments, you internalize the motivational patterns, then seek situations where you fit the best.

This cycle can be broken and changed, but typically only when it is interrupted by new experiences in the other five personality regions. If you are a performer, you might, for example, mistakenly marry a commander. This would disrupt your performer patterns and increase your needs to command, as you would pressure your spouse to learn to perform. Similarly, you might undergo significant changes by working for a boss who is an attacker. You might learn new forms of behavior by training, therapy, significant failures or successes, or other shocking experiences. A severe heart attack often changes executives drastically. New, contradictory motivational environments are the producers of change. Most people, however, prefer not to get into new, change-producing environments. Consequently, their early acquired motivational needs go unaltered. Active people, leaders and executives, generally have little choice in the matter, however, for often they are forced to face new contradictory environments. Thus, they change more than most. We will now look at each of these needs more precisely.

The Distribution of Personality Types

My research suggests only about 8 percent of our population are achievers, and thus, are truly psychologically healthy and most effective as leaders. (See Chart 1.)

You notice in Chart 1 that the percentage of achievers increases dramatically in the higher levels of organizations. This gives testimony to their overall health and effectiveness in dealing with others. Also, notice that the number of avoiders, pleasers, and attackers drop sharply in the higher levels of administration. Indeed, their personalities are not proper matches for the demands of these complex jobs.

One point is very clear; we are a *performer society*. This per-

Chart 1

ESTIMATES OF PERCENTAGES IN EACH
PERSONALITY TYPE*

	% General Population	% Middle Level Administrators and Managers	% Top Level Administrators and Managers
Commander	16	18	22
Attacker	8	6	4
Avoider	20	9	3
Pleaser	14	11	5
Performer	35	42	41
Achiever	8	14	24

*Based on a sample of 3,000 people from a wide variety of occupations, social classes, education, religions, IQ, and parts of the country. People were ranked based on their dominant need only.

sonality type pervades our institutions—business, education, medicine, the arts, government, family, religion. Another, and perhaps more distinctive point, is that 24 percent of all top leaders are achievers. He clearly outdistances the performer and the commander in this regard.

The prevalence of different personality types, however, varies with the type of institution. In banking about 60 percent of those at the level of vice-president or above are performers because performer skills are a primary requisite for their work. On the other hand, upper levels of manufacturing and technical firms contain only about 25 percent performers, but contain 55 percent commanders. These technologies reward precision and order. Similarly, clerical jobs in banking, insurance firms, universities, hospitals, and other organizations possess up to 70 percent avoiders and pleasers. These jobs allow the avoider to hide. Mass production jobs also are made up of many avoiders—around 60 percent. Jobs vary, then, according to how well they reward different personality types.

There are a higher percentage of women in the avoider and pleaser categories than men because they have been brought up in these patterns. The women's movement is fighting to overcome this and, indeed, there seems to be a significant decline among younger women in the avoider and pleaser categories.

Caution in the Use of Categories to Label Personality

Do not become upset with terms used to refer to the six psychological needs. There is no magic in the particular words I have chosen. I could have selected different labels or even numbers. I tried to choose those names, however, which most accurately reflect the essence of each personality. The labels are not as important as the actual characteristics of the personality types, for it is the latter which gives meaning to the labels in the long run. The label commander, for instance, was selected to connote a person who likes to command others in an orderly way. The term performer, similarly, was chosen to reflect an actor and a producer.

How to Use This Typology of Six Personality Types

Many psychologists strongly reject the use of typologies—classification based on types—such as the one I develop in this book. They argue that typologies encourage the view of people as stereotypes rather than as individuals. However, a typology does not fix a person in a category—people who use the typology do. Typologies are extremely important in communicating and analyzing individuals, and they should be used as flexible, open tools. We should use them, but wisely.

Individuals are dynamic; they change, and are constantly in process. They are not static. In addition, each person is profoundly unique. To develop a perfectly accurate typology, we would need millions of types, and even then we would have to change them daily since people change. Any typology short of this is not perfect for all individuals, but to develop a typology with millions of categories is not practical or useful. Thus, my typology of six basic psychological needs, while clearly not perfect, has been extremely useful to me and others in understanding and in helping people.

A good way to think about personality and how we understand

DIAGRAM 2

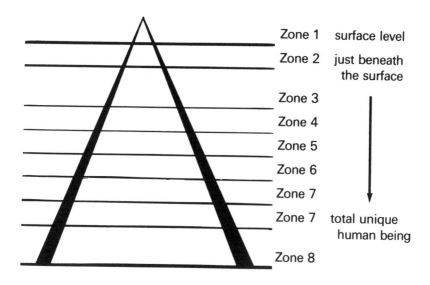

Zone 1   surface level

Zone 2   just beneath
         the surface

Zone 3

Zone 4

Zone 5

Zone 6

Zone 7

Zone 7   total unique
         human being

Zone 8

it is to imagine a person's total being—his person—as an iceberg. The part of his unique person that is above water (Zone 1) is what is seen in casual conversations, in discussions, on the phone, or in large group meetings. What is typically seen in most relationships with people is on this level and reveals only a small part of the total person.

Zone 2 is just beneath the surface and typically is discovered by more intimate contact with a person. Work associates, friends, secretaries, and close neighbors often fall into our Zone 2 knowledge area. You know a little more about their unique personalities than you do about more casual acquaintances. I have found that the typology presented here deals with Zones 4, 5, and 6. If you can truly rank a person according to the degree of these six needs or types he possesses, then I think you have aimed at an extremely good, although not complete, understanding of him. The final depths (Zones 7 and 8) of a person's personality can only be comprehended,

I believe, by intensive personal lengthy psychological diagnosis by a skillful, experienced expert (he need not necessarily be a psychologist or psychiatrist).

My experience has been that most people reach only Zones 1 and 2 in their relationships. This causes most individuals to homogenize others, to see all people as being about the same, to miss the significant individual differences. Consequently, most individuals have difficulty analyzing and understanding the deeper motivations, needs, and personality characteristics, that are discussed here.[4] By mastering the concepts presented in *The Achievers*, you hopefully will gain an increased skill in understanding yourself and others. But remember to use these personality models wisely. Change your rankings as you gain new insights. Alter your diagnosis as the person changes. Try not to use these six models blindly as rigid stereotypes. Let them assist you, not restrict you. Let these six personality concepts guide you, not bind you. Let them help you, not block you from understanding yourself and others.

Many of my colleagues in humanistic, clinical, and therapeutic psychology have their own typologies, but they are hidden or implicit in their therapeutic styles and goals. It has been helpful for me, however, to try to make my assumptions and models of man explicit so that I can deal with them in working with others and myself. I have been able to improve my theories the more I am open to them. I have been able to help others better the more I understand myself and them. These six models of personality will hopefully help you to do the same.

This book is divided into two main parts. The first is an analysis of the six major psychological needs. The second is devoted to how to apply these needs in leadership roles, close relationships, and family activities.

Exercise to Accompany Part 1

You will be able to use the ideas presented in *The Achievers* best if you do the following exercise before reading further. First, write

---

4. I have found, for example, that the great majority of individuals rate themselves very highly on their skills in dealing with others. Their friends and associates, however, sharply disagree with their self-evaluations.

down the names of the ten people you know best. Your list can include your spouse, children, parents, friends, work associates, or others. They should be people you know very well. The reason for ranking ten people is to ensure enough variety to be able to apply all six personality types. You must know them well to understand them[5]. Second, tear out Chart Two so you can keep it private. This will ensure honesty in evaluating your friends. Third, try to rank each of the ten people you have listed, plus yourself, on the six personality needs. Try to do this now. You may, however, do this while reading the chapters. Rank each person on what you think his most dominant need is. Place a 1 under his most dominant need. Then place a 2 under his secondary or next most dominant personality factor. Give a 3 to this third most dominant characteristic, and so on until you reach 6. This exercise will help you make these six psychological needs come to life, and will enable you to understand your close associates and your own motivations more thoroughly.

As you read through the next chapters please refer to your list frequently; readjust your rankings as you gain new insights and keep examining yourself carefully. The facts are valuable.

How do you feel right now about completing Chart One: The Achievement Study Guide? *Avoiders* often say when asked to do this exercise, "It really doesn't matter, it won't help. What's the use!! I don't have time." *Achievers* usually respond, "It sounds interesting and probably worthwhile. I'll experiment, take a risk, and try it." *Pleasers* typically say, "All my friends are nice people. How could I be so critical to judge them?" *Attackers* say, "Boy, this is a good exercise to use to get those goons. I must be an achiever because I can see them clearly—as dummies." *Commanders* react, "Now how exactly do I do this? Is this what I am supposed to do? If I do it, I'll do it precisely," And, *Performers* respond, "If I can learn better how to manipulate people I can get ahead. I'll try it maybe."

---

5. I have found that most people do not know many individuals well. If this applies to you, you must make an effort to study people to be able to understand them.

Chart 2

THE ACHIEVEMENT STUDY GUIDE

The Six Types of Personalities

NAMES	Commander	Attacker	Avoider	Pleaser	Performer	Achiever
1. Bob	3	2				1
2. John						
3.						
4.						
5.						
6.						
7.						
8.						
9.						
10.						
YOURSELF						

Try to use this chart with each chapter. You will find it difficult to rank people at first, but keep trying and you will discover that people tend to fall into these categories as you gain skill in analyzing their motivations. Be sure to ask why they do what they do as well as to observe what they do. If you use this exercise actively, my experience indicates you will gain significant insights into others' motivations as well as into your own. Accordingly, you will become more effective and satisfied.

CHAPTER 2

The Commander

His friends call him "Bullet Billy." His real name is Billy Long. Billy, a senior member of a successful California law firm, acquired his nickname because his partners marveled at his strong will. One colleague remarked, "He can 'bite the bullet' as it speeds in on him; he can face a client squarely and squash him. He is made of steel."

Billy's legal work is outstandingly organized, precise and detailed. In law school, for three years Billy studied constantly, according to an exacting regimen. He had one simple purpose: to do things right or not at all. His new wife (he married his high school sweetheart) faithfully devoted herself to supporting Billy's rigid routines. In his law firm, Billy has become a demanding workhorse. Seldom, if ever, does an undotted, "i" escape his notice. He makes quick decisions. He remembers legal precedents most others had long forgotten. His preparations for a case are notoriously thorough. Yet, in the courtroom, Billy follows his defense plan to a fault, because he often disregards new and unexpected evidence. He lost several major cases, in fact, because he did not react creatively to unforeseen developments in the course of the trials. In the firm's coffee lounge, the young lawyers quickly mute their conversation whenever Billy walks in. They are struck with awe and fear, yet they have admiration and respect for Billy. One trainee said, "Whatever we do with Bullet Billy we never call him that to his face—you had better listen carefully and take notes or you'll find yourself in serious jeopardy."

Do you know someone like Billy? Do you know someone who is bossy and rigid? Select the person who comes to mind as the most autocratic, organized person you know, then write his initials here. This will provide you with a live model with which to compare the descriptions of the commander.

What are the main characteristics of the person you have selected? What kind of jobs does he perform most effectively? How warm and relaxed is he? How does he react when you disagree with him? What kind of upbringing did he have? These questions are answered in this chapter. There are nine basic characteristics of the commander. To gain insights into these characteristics, it is most helpful to study first how the commander became so domineering and orderly.

The Commander is Shaped by a Demanding and Orderly Environment[1]

The commander's parents and his other socializing experiences—at school, with his peers, on the job—often complement each other in an unusual manner. Classically, in the case of his parents, one is a commander and the other an avoider. If his father is the commander he makes all decisions for the child that affect his life and determine his beliefs. The father teaches him how to think, feel, and behave.

The commander parent sets high goals for his child and pushes him hard to accomplish them. He does this by one method: downward communication. Two-way communication does not exist. Consequently, he controls the destiny of his child in a very strict and orderly way. It is as if the father drilled holes in his child's head, inserted clear-cut ideas, and closed them up again.

Billy Long's father—a military base commander who became the mayor, leading citizen, and elder authority figure of his small

---

1. I am assuming that most of one's early childhood, adolescent and adult experiences have a significant impact on the development of one's personality. We learn most of our motivations and needs from our early stimulations, rewards, and punishments in our families. Later peer and adult experiences, however, often modify these learnings extensively. This suggests that personality needs can and do change over time as a result of environmental and situational changes.

Certainly man's total being is a result of his genetic and biochemical interaction with his psychological make-up. In my judgment, however, the personality needs evolve more as a result of interaction with parents, peers, siblings, jobs, cultural, and other environmental stimulations than from biological causes.

California town when he retired—gave his son anything as long as he did what he was told. For example, he gave him a brand new car when he was 16. Billy had to observe strict and regular church attendance, quiet piety all day Sunday, and complete abstinence from alcohol, tobacco, and profanity.

The difference between the commander parent and the achiever parent can be made clear with the following example. If a commander father, for example, wanted his sixteen-year-old daughter to deliver a package for him from downtown Manhattan to Long Island, he would tell her exactly how to get there by specifying each turn, stop light, bridge and direction. By contrast, an achiever father would discuss the trip with her, say "I know you can make it on your own. If you need any help, call me." The achiever daughter might well drive for miles in the wrong direction, get lost several times, and arrive late. After several trips to Long Island, however, the achiever daughter eventually would arrive at the same "correct path" the commander father directed his daughter to follow.

What do you think both girls would do at this point if, on the next trip, one of the bridges were down? The achiever would say, "Well, I'll just go on one of the alternative paths I've traveled before—no problem." She would rely on her own skill. The commander would be likely to call home for instructions, retrace her steps, or sit in her car and wait for help. This example contrasts the ways the commander and achiever learn to think. The commander is taught the answers, ones that fit specific categories, while the achiever acquires answers by trial and error, by self-experience. This latter process takes longer for the achiever, but it is more thorough. It is a process of self-discovery and self-learning, as opposed to the forced learning of the commander.

The commander parent does not allow conflicts. When they do occur spontaneously, they are quickly smothered: "We won't talk about that any more." "You will get your hair cut and that's that." "Children are to be seen and not heard." Soon the commander's child learns that he is rewarded for conforming to his parent's standards of conduct and punished for deviating from them. As a result, the child learns to view his world in clear-cut categories. He becomes self-disciplined, always remains under control, keeps his distance from others, plans and organizes his relationships carefully.

Now, you are probably wondering, "How could a child who was

raised in such a strict environment become domineering himself? Wouldn't he become meek and passive?'' I, too, was long confused by this apparent dilemma until I suddenly asked, ''What kind of spouse would a commander be most likely to marry? Who would be the most compatible with him?'' The answer is not surprising. He prefers an avoider!

An avoider mother typically overindulges her child. The child, consequently, ends up dominating his mother! She relates to her child in the same way she does to her husband and her friends— subserviently. She needs to be directed. She asks her son, for example, ''What would you like for breakfast?'' He replies, ''scrambled eggs.'' As she serves them he might well knock them off the table and demand pancakes. The mother, quite willing, returns to the kitchen to produce a new menu. As one executive I know told me, ''My mother used to sneak into my bedroom when I was a little boy and pull the covers off my feet and put on my socks and shoes so I could have a few extra minutes in the mornings before I went to school.'' I could never quite figure how he got his pants on, but as he commented, ''you know, I almost grew up thinking I was God. I could boss these great big people around.'' Likewise, Billy Long's mother listened for his every breath and jumped to satisfy his whims. She was a timid but tender woman. Often, however, she complained of illness in the absence of any visible symptoms; but this got her husband's and son's attention.

The commander's father, then, teaches him his desire for order, precision and self-control; his mother creates his need to dominate and to seek power. The father supports his need for power, and the mother adds some fear of failing to his motivational mix. Warmth, easy laughter, and spontaneous friendships are neither encouraged nor molded by either parent. Consequently, as he matures, the child becomes rigid in his beliefs and cold in his interpersonal relationships.

A child's peers, school, siblings and, later, his job also mold his psychological needs. If, for instance, you work for a commander boss a long time, he will have great influence upon your personality needs. If you attend a school that is run in a commander style, your personality will be molded in its image. Ultimately, of course, your motivations are the combined result of your parents' influences and these other forces.

Usually, however, your parents' training patterns are significantly related to your experience outside the family. Commander parents are likely to prefer (1) schools and teachers for their children that are strict and orderly, like military school, (2) playmates who are being reared in a similar commander style, and (3) churches, recreational and social exposures that are rigid and disciplined.

After many years of indoctrination in the need to command, a person seeks out situations, jobs, and friends that are compatible environments—that support his need to command. He might well select a spouse who is an avoider and a career that allows him to be orderly and domineering. Although he is not successful all the time in selecting his preferred commander environment, he moves steadily toward commander situations.

Many scholars, Freudians for example, would disagree with my explanations of how the commander acquired his personality characteristics. My research suggests they are valid. Nevertheless, if you prefer a different explanation, this does not necessarily interfere with your acceptance and understanding of the behavior of the commander (or other five) personality systems. We will focus now on the commander's nine personality characteristics.

The Commander Is Domineering

Because of his particular style of upbringing, the commander is very domineering and autocratic. He exerts his strength at every opportunity. He sees power and control as the most important aspects of his life. One apparent commander wrote the following story about the picture that appears in chapter 1 of a group of people sitting around a table:

> The boss has just told these men that he completed plans for the implementation of a new system for regulating their production operations. They have had a problem with slack time and a large inventory. Now they will be able to control all of the factors that have been causing confusion. They are saying how wonderful it is going to be to have precision placed back into the work force. The men on the line are going to have to follow our standards or go.

An elementary school teacher who had a high need to command wrote this story about the same picture:

The principal is standing and telling the other teachers the plans for the new curriculum which he is going to install next semester. The other teachers are impressed with how well thought-out the schedules are.

One subordinate of a commander said, "Man I want to tell you that you always know where your bread is buttered with this guy. You go along with him or else. There are two ways to do things— his way and the wrong way. He even looks at you with an authoritarian glare. It's just not worth it to argue with him because you always end up losing. He overpowers you."

The commander controls his environment so he can regulate the events he encounters and make them predictable. By dominating people and situations he can successfully apply his rigid categories of thinking, maintain his self-control, and follow his parental models for power and order. A top vice-president (a man with extreme commander needs) of a West Coast conglomerate demonstrated this point. He had all the legs on the chairs in his conference room except his, cut one-half inch. He confided to me: "I did this so I could command a position of respect with my subordinates."

Because the commander dominates others, he appears quite intelligent, sure of himself, and competent; thus, when he is correct in his decisions, his authority is reinforced. When errors occur, however, he blames mistakes on faulty implementation by subordinates. He rarely admits making a wrong decision. Consequently, his errors often go unnoticed. Since the alternatives to his decisions are seldom open for discussion, they are not usually visible. Thus, he may commit numerous "invisible errors," yet appear more intelligent than he actually is.[2]

The Commander Uses Categorical Thinking

As mentioned earlier, the commander's parents raised him by drilling ideas into his head: "You should never drink." "Always say, 'Yes, sir.'" "Thank you ma'am." "You should always be on time, go to church, clean up your room." This "drilling process"

2. Harold Leavitt's experiments with one-way and two-way communications illustrate these points vividly. (*Managerial Psychology*, Chicago: University of Chicago Press, 1969.)

leaves the child with clean-cut categories of beliefs. He perceives his world, therefore, through "categorical" eyes. He acquires a fixed set of answers for all situations. Things are either good or bad, right or wrong, black or white, either/or. People, ideas, and events either fit into one of his drilled holes or they do not. If they do, he thinks they are great. If they do not, they are rejected. When I mentioned this point to the assistant director of a hospital one evening, he excitedly remarked,

> I know an obvious commander (my boss, a man possessed) who constantly uses militaristic phrases like "stand by" on the phone, or "got you covered," or "all the troops are in the shop." I wonder if you're not overlooking the richest source of analysis—the military mind. Does your chair-cutting commander, for example, think like a colonel?

Indeed, the military, more so in the past, is a breeding ground for many of the commander qualities.

The process of categorical thinking is reflected further in the commander's use of precise words. Only rarely will you hear him say "maybe, perhaps, I wonder, possibly"; rather he states, "This is the way to do it," "Definitely," "Precisely," "Exactly," "Certainly."

Similarly, since he lives by a large number of rigid categories, the commander develops a phenomenal memory which helps him react to sudden or novel events. By storing facts, he is less often surprised.

An interesting example of how the commander applies his rigid categories to his environment occurred when Hank Thompson, an obvious commander, took over the presidency of a large midwestern food business. One of the company's vice-presidents said:

> Since he took over he has eliminated each tailor-made marketing and advertising program that had been especially designed for our different product lines and market segments. We now have "one best way" that covers everything. He's put all the products into one big pot. He's like Henry Ford but fifty years late with one best car, one color, price, and so forth. The local markets are screaming, because what works in New York doesn't apply to Texas. He runs his field force the same way. They all report directly to him, fill out 1000 forms and do it all according to his book.

The commander's categorical thinking patterns cause him great difficulty in perceiving subtle differences between ideas, people, and events. He forms conclusions quickly since he prejudges them according to his stereotyped ideas. One elementary school teacher described her commander principal by saying, "She always tries to solve each new problem we have with the same old solutions. Even though she knows they haven't worked before, she'll just go on making us do it her way, because that's the way we've always done it!"

The commander is not a creative person, but he is an implementer of ideas, an organizer and director of activities. He does not see the fresh or unique as the achiever does. He only sees the stereotyped and traditional. Because the commander sees the world in clear-cut categories, he has difficulty assuming the role of another person. If asked, "How do you think John feels about this new move?" he is unable to put himself into John's shoes, or to imagine how John feels. Instead, he thinks in concrete terms about what he calls "hard facts." Feelings, or as he puts it, "soft, fuzzy thinking," are very difficult for him to understand, so he rejects them as unacceptable. Neither a theoretician nor a philosopher, he conceptualizes only specific examples, not abstractions. Consequently, he hates the ambiguities, uncertainties and novelties inherent in, for instance, a committee's efforts to formulate a unique plan or to develop an idea. Likewise, a commander mother cannot imagine how her child feels. She does not see the unique qualities of each child or relate to each one in a differentiate fashion. A commander nurse, too, has formulas that guide his routine; he follows these to the letter.

Because he thinks in fixed stereotypes, the commander does not examine new ideas or explore for alternatives. He does not look for multiple causes for events (Milton Rokeach, *The Open and Closed Mind*, 1960). Instead of searching for unique approaches, he follows his fixed ideas. If they do not work, he simply stops. He does not experiment readily with new ways of improving his performance. A commander mother may say, for example, "I am going to raise my children by the book and that's that." Experimentation is not her forte. Billy Long, for example, married the girl he first dated. He did not date a variety of women or try to discover what he was looking for in a wife.

The Commander Sees Only One Aspect of Communication

The commander has difficulty perceiving the two-part nature of communication—(1) the logic of the message, (2) the personal image, or values of the speaker. The more authority a speaker has, for example, the more the commander will be influenced by the personal image of the speaker rather than by the logic of his message.

An interesting example of this was revealed by a rather courageous and playful army private, Tom, whose sergeant was a commander. Tom arrived for his first day of summer camp to find he was scheduled for duty at 5:00 A.M. each morning. The first morning he strolled in at 7:30. The sergeant was furious. He barked, ''Where have you been?'' Tom replied, ''Well, he sent me over there to move those boxes first.'' The sergeant looked surprised. His jaw dropped. He stood with a puzzled look on his face, mumbled something to himself, but finally said, ''Okay, get to work!''

The next morning Tom again arrived for duty about 7:30. Again the sergeant greeted Tom with hands on hips and a stern grimace on his face. He inquired loudly: ''Where were you?'' Tom replied in earnest tones: ''Well, he told me to work over there again this morning.'' ''Who told you?'' asked the sergeant. Tom said, ''You know,'' pointing to his shoulders where rank is typically indicated, ''him.'' The sergeant stared at Tom for several seconds longer, then said, ''Okay, let's get going!''

This commander sergeant had merely popped Tom's communication into a prejudged storage bin—if any authority said do it, it must be okay. He didn't bother to inquire further. This case illustrates that the commander often gets fooled because of his blind spots for power. His perception is distorted by his reverence for those in authority and his concern for following orders.

The Commander Is Closed-Minded

A commander's categorical thinking patterns also cause him to be very close-minded. In a seminar for wives of executives, one woman said,

My husband is as stubborn as a mule. No matter what you say, he won't change his mind. You can argue like the dickens and have a real good point, but he won't give an inch. Later on he might come back and say he has an idea and just repeat yours. As long as he can think it was his thought, he'll buy it, but otherwise, forget it.

Since the commander is uncomfortable with ideas he does not understand or control, he resists change and innovative thought, but later adopts them under his own name so he can demonstrate his control.

His opposition to change is exemplified by a commander who planned a vacation which required driving across the country. He designed a precise schedule for each gas stop, the time and place for every meal, and all the overnight accommodations. During the trip, he followed the plan rigidly no matter what occurred along the way. Even if his family needed to go to the bathroom at a non-scheduled moment or complained about the schedule, he adamantly refused to change his plans. If his wife asked why, he replied: ''Well, ah, because it is just better to do it this way.'' The real reason for his obstinance, of course, was to satisfy his need for order and control.

The Commander Is Self-Disciplined

The commander is extraordinarily self-controlled because of his drilled upbringing. The achiever, by contrast, allows complexity and disorder into his perceptions and is not made very anxious by the chaos he sees in life.

A commander designs his life according to schedules, rules, and unbreakable routines. A patterned life makes him happy. Uncertainty makes him nervous; therefore, he demands precise discussions and assignments. When he finds himself in a confusing situation, he has an overwhelming urge to force it into his standard categories of thinking. Consequently, he frequently makes impulsive decisions just to clear up the uncertainty, even if it produces poor results, for he would rather be certain than to be right. He would rather be efficient than effective.

When a commander is confronted by a confusing situation, he often reacts hostilely under the stress of uncertainty. This reaction may take the form of screaming, pounding tables, or other temperamental releases. If the confusion is prolonged and there is no escape from the ambiguity, he may literally experience a breakdown. When he is out of control, he becomes helpless.

To keep his composure when surrounded by uncertainty, the commander maintains a rigid, cold posture in his relationships. In describing his commander president, the marketing director for a large electronics firm commented,

> You really can't get close to him. Even if you give him a warm, personal compliment for something he's done, he gets red in the face and then brushes you off. Many times I've seen him make an aggressive joke when someone shows him affection, just to get them away. He's a complex man. You know he means well, but you just don't get close to him.

Usually his files, desk and office are in immaculate order. Most of the routines of his job are highly systematized. His secretary comments, "Boy, if you leave something out of place you'd better watch it. He likes his things kept neat. If you mess them up, he blows his stack."

Similarly, the commander as a homemaker keeps his house in perfect order and his life under control. When his friends put out a cigarette, he hustles the ashtray off to the kitchen before the guests leave. His food is neatly stored; the children follow fixed routines.

The Commander Has A Routine Sexual Style

The commander's sexual style—how he makes love—reflects his self-discipline.[3] My personal interviews and counseling with commanders and their spouses reveal their sexual relationships to be hygienically rigid. One rather frustrated wife of a commander complained,

> He assigns every Wednesday night and Sunday afternoon for intercourse. We go through the same routine everytime. He closes the

---

3. I have studied 148 individuals' sexual style in relationship to their personality types. Because the number of each personality type is so small, these conclusions are tentative.

doors, checks the locks, takes a shower, and brushes his teeth. He gets on top and we're finished. It's like making love with a machine.

Medicinal sex is the commander's goal, for by regulating his deeper emotions and feelings, he keeps his life under control. He views sexual intercourse as a physical release, not as a sharing of deep love. One husband of a commander commented, "My wife isn't very expressive. She doesn't hug, touch or kiss. She thinks sex is sex, and has nothing to do with how you feel about another person.

The Commander Performs Well in Orderly Situations

The commander is a hard worker who expends an enormous amount of effort to attain his goals. By exerting himself, he ensures his ability to dominate others and to control unpredictable events. Similarly, since he is highly committed to his goals because they were drilled into him, he eagerly works to prove their value and to ensure that others acquire his beliefs.

The commander prefers jobs, games, and hobbies which encourage precision and detail. He favors technical training but opposes interpersonal skill training, t-groups, or other such "nonsense."

He is good at managing firms with routine technologies such as textiles or automobile assembly lines because his demand for precision fits nicely with the detailed efficiency required from production schedules and inventory controls. The technologies of bookkeeping and computer operations are also compatible with the commander's personality. He excels at tasks which depend on careful planning, detailed supervision, and exacting organization. But when there is a need for creative solutions, flexibility, spontaneity, and effective interpersonal relationships, he performs poorly.

The Commander Sets High Goals and Takes Below-Average Risks

Although the commander sets high goals for himself, he takes few risks—slightly more than an avoider would take, and somewhat fewer than a performer or achiever. The commander, for example, may set as his personal goal the production of 50,000 yards of fiber per hour. To do this, he must work hard, concentrating steadily for long hours. He knows he can reach 50,000 yards per hour if he applies himself. This goal does not require special decisions or creative solutions, but rather discipline and hard work. Thus his goal is high in quantity, for few people reach it; but it involves little risk.

A riskier goal is one that includes more unknown qualities, leads to unpredictable events, and demands unique solutions. "Qualitatively risky" goals involve such decisions as whether to change jobs, market a new product, hire one executive over another, enter a new territory, or send a child to one school instead of another.

The contrast between "quantity goals" and "quality goals" was illustrated clearly in an advertising firm owned by two partners. One partner was a performer, the other a commander. The business had grown profitably during its eight years of existence. In a long-range planning conference I attended with these men, they were trying to plan the firm's business strategy for the next five years. The performer kept suggesting new innovations that would carry fifty-fifty degrees of risk—exciting but realistic goals. The commander was quite concerned with this line of reasoning. He said, "Why do you want to go off in all those different directions? Sure, the return on investment might be great, but if we marshal our people and instill more exacting standards, I know we can increase our profit by 25 percent next year by just continuing to do the things we're doing now, but much better."

By no means was the commander trying to get out of work or to slow down. In fact, he was urging higher standards of performance, greater commitment and more difficult goals for their firm, but he wanted to follow a predictable, proven path, not a risky one.

This process is very much like the commander football coach who works his team to death, gets them in super shape, drives them to perfection in carrying out each assignment, and has a very simple offense and defense. "Three yards and a cloud of dust, hit to hurt, go after the man with the ball," are his strategies. This, of course, is contrasted by the performer team that has much "razzle-dazzle," variety and more risky plays on both offense and defense. Both teams may work hard, have very high goals, yet take different degrees of risk.

Another fascinating portrayal of this difference was demonstrated in the early years of General Motors as contrasted with Ford. Under

William Durante's leadership in the 1900s, GM moved flexibly and introduced a great variety of products and innovations. GM managers were more achievement-oriented, risk-takers. Ford, however, had one best car, color, price, and assembly line. Variation was almost forbidden, yet employees worked hard toward extremely high goals of output and perfection (Alfred P. Sloan, Jr., *My Years with General Motors*, 1963). Both companies succeeded but by following quite different means. In addition, each firm had serious problems which resulted from these differences. GM, in its early years, almost went broke because of confusion. Ford almost died because of rigidity.

The Commander Has Moderate Psychological Health

Even when he is in an orderly situation that he can dominate, and thus, feel most comfortable in, he is far from self-contentment. He is quite tense, anxious, and nervous. To him, feelings are to be hidden; consequently, he suppresses his inner life. He is seldom spontaneous, for rigid control of his normal impulses is his overpowering concern.

In his relations with others, a commander displays his lack of self-confidence by his cold, impersonal manner. He seldom genuinely smiles, and "belly laughs" are utterly foreign to his behavior. His stiffness and rigidity indicate that he is uncomfortable with himself and mistrusts his abilities. The variety of life, which continually confronts most of us, frightens him. The commander's life is more a duty than a pleasure.

The commander has an unclear, awkward self-concept. When you ask him to describe what he is like, he will give you short, unconnected descriptions of his major traits. He does not see the full range of his strengths and weaknesses, the subtle complexities of his personality or how he acquired them. He sees himself as good or bad, smart or dumb, ambitious or lazy.

The commander also holds many beliefs that are completely contradictory. Often he does not realize it. He might state, for example, "I believe in democracy, liberty and justice for all. People everywhere should participate in the politics of the country." Then say, "Those damn young rebels should be chained, whipped, and shipped out of the country." The commander can have such contradictory beliefs because his values were drilled into him, they were not acquired systematically or thoughtfully. Positive self-worth for commanders, therefore, becomes synonymous with conformity to externally prescribed rules and codes of conduct, not with self-determined standards of behavior.

The commander then, has moderate—about 50 percent—self-confidence. His self-acceptance is not as low as the avoider's nor as high as the achiever's. He gains some satisfaction from being self-assertive and moderately successful. Yet, even when he is in a domineering position, he does not reach much self-acceptance, because he is not genuinely open, aware, or self-reliant. He feels he must be constantly on guard even when things are going smoothly, for the unpredictable is always lurking in the background. This makes him nervous and tense.

By contrast achievers have a much better opinion of themselves. They use more favorable adjectives in self-descriptions, make higher scores on self-acceptance tests, and are willing to speak more openly and thus more critically about themselves. Commanders make average scores in these three areas, while avoiders, who have the lowest psychological health and are least open to their own feelings, emotions, and their ''inner life,'' score lowest. For these reasons, I rank the commander as 50 percent psychologically healthy.[4] The commander's strengths are his aggressiveness and self-discipline. He gains results, is quite productive and derives satisfaction from reaching his goals in an organized fashion. He is moderately self-contained, has average desires to learn and to improve, and is often courageous when faced with severe difficulties, for he has strength to persevere to fulfill his wishes.

SUMMARY

You will find it helpful now to look back at the list of ten friends you ranked in chapter 1. Which person has the highest need to command? How well do the previous traits fit him? Was the person

---

4. This rank is merely a score to indicate the comparison between the six different personality types. There is no magic in the figure 50 percent. It indicates, rather, that the commander is only half as healthy as the achiever, but about twice as healthy as the attacker, and even more so than the avoider!

you thought of in response to the questions at the beginning of this chapter pure commander? How much of the need to command do you have?

To refresh your thinking about the major characteristics of a commander, you will learn the most and fit the previous ideas into your own thoughts more effectively if you take an active role by trying to recall the nine major traits of the commander. Please outline these characteristics below to provide your own summary of the chapter.

1. Domineering
2. Uses Categorical thinking
3. One aspect of communication
4. Closed Minded
5. Self Disciplined
6. Routine Sexual Style
7. Performs Well in Orderly Situations
8. Sets High goals takes Below Avg Risk
9. Moderate psychological health

CHAPTER 3

The Attacker

Dick Benton's office was barren. Other than the title on his door which labeled him vice-president of mergers and acquisitions there were no pictures, souvenirs, books or photographs that revealed his character. Sterile walls and metal office furniture greeted the major stockholders of a small, New England real estate development company who had arrived in Chicago to interview Dick for the presidency of their future firm.

Dick opened the conversation by asking, "What can you possibly offer me? I make $55,000 a year, have a stock option that will make a millionaire by the time I retire in fifteen years. You are a minor little business in a backward area of New England."

The spokesman for the group gently explained, "Our firm is small, but we have great potential to develop ski resort and leisure-type property. Most of us who founded the firm, however, are all near retirement, and we do not have the experience nor energy to expand into large investments. We want a top man to take our company, with our financial backing, and make it grow."

The stockholders were perplexed, yet impressed with Dick. After further interviews they decided to offer the job to him, even though they had many reservations about his abrasive manner. They had experienced such difficulty in bargaining with Dick that they assumed he would be a fierce competitor, and this is what they assumed was needed in big-time real estate development.

During the first six months of Dick's leadership, he fired four of the seven top officers of the firm, caused eight salesmen to quit, and four of the five original founders and major stockholders to sell out and resign from the company. He did this by angrily accusing them of trying to prevent him from taking over active leadership, calling them names, and making indecent passes at their wives.

One officer of the firm explained his exodus by saying,

> I don't know exactly what it is, but he would call me to discuss some normal business situation and within three minutes he would be cutting me apart. I would get mad and we'd end up yelling. When he made that last sales call with me and told my old customer, who I greatly respected, that he was a stupid ass, I knew this company wasn't for me anymore.

Similarly, one of the founders of the company remarked,

> We discovered five months after Dick Benton took over the presidency that the three recommendations we received on him were all falsified. Dick had given us the names of three key people in his past jobs; he had jumped around a lot, then twisted each one's arm to make sure he came out good. He got the secretary of one of his past employers to intercept our call and say, "My boss cannot be reached for a long time but I can give you all the information you need on Dick Benton." She then painted a false, positive picture of him. Dick told the other two people that if they didn't give him a great recommendation he would really get them. So, they told us only half truths. After these last six months I can understand why they would be afraid of him. Interestingly, he is known in the company now as "terrible Dick."

Do you know someone like terrible Dick Benton? Think of the person you know who is the most antagonistic, cynical, and rebellious and write in his initials here so you can keep him in mind as you read this chapter. S M_____

To help you understand the person you just selected—the attacker—think how you feel when you are in a bad mood—grumpy, upset, tense and anxious. This is how the attacker feels most of the time and he behaves accordingly; he is bitter and defiant.

In *One Flew Over the Cuckoo's Nest*, Ken Kesey delivers a frighteningly vivid portrayal of an attacker, the "Big Nurse." She enjoys herself by psychologically "castrating" her patients. "She slides through the door with a gust of cold and locks the door behind her," Kesey wrote; As the Big Nurse approaches the black hospital attendants who did not hear her enter the hallway, "she goes into a crouch and advances. . . . I can see she's furious, clean out of control. She's going to tear the black bastards limb from limb, she's so furious" (pp. 3–4).

The attacker is at war with the world. One sales trainee described his attacker boss this way:

> The first day I went to work he said to me, "Fella, you will never sell anything until you learn one simple thing. The man on the other side of the counter is the enemy." It was a gladiator's school we were in . . . strife was honored . . . openly. Combat was the ideal— combat with the dealer, combat with the 'chiselling competitors,' combat with each other. (David McClelland, *The Achieving Society*, 1961, p. 270)

The Attacker Is Shaped by a Domineering, Inconsistent and Harsh Environment

The parents of the attacker, as well as his major social, work, and peer-group experiences, aggressively and punitively mold the child. Whereas the commander's parents are domineering and orderly, the attacker's parents—typically both the husband and wife are attackers—are inconsistent, contradictory, and harsh. One day they urge him to study for good grades. The next day they ridicule him for being a bookworm. They feel they can best make their child "knuckle under" if they severely punish him when he deviates from their wishes.

One of my patients dramatically demonstrated this inconsistency and harshness by overindulging her two-year-old son on the one hand and force-feeding him on the other. She made his favorite cookies and placed them by his bed so he could eat them when he woke up at night. Yet, at meal times she literally stuffed food down his mouth by holding his nose so he would eat what she wanted. Interestingly, this child at the age of 3, was mean and rebellious. He had been kicked out of two nursery schools, run through a dozen baby sitters and earned a reputation on his block for being the one "you don't let your kid play with." He got so mad at his parents, for example, for not allowing him to go outside and play in the summer that he broke through the screen door.

Similarly, by the age of three and one-half, the child was so aggressive that he broke his crib by banging his head against it. He refused to be kissed or hugged, frequently holding his breath until he turned blue to get his way. His parents retaliated by slapping him until he cried. Scolding this baby attacker for being hyperactive, they reinforced his aggressive behavior.

Because parents' directions are painfully contradictory and stinging, the attacker views his rewards and punishments as arbitrary.[1] One teen-aged attacker told me:

> I soon learned that it really didn't matter what I did, just whether it happened to strike my parents' fancy at the time. So, I said "the hell with what they say. It doesn't have any importance." I'm afraid it has made me bitter against all people who try to tell me what to do. I can be driving down the street, see a policeman and just want to run over him. It is like a natural impulse. It just happens automatically. The hair on my neck goes up when people get too bossy.

Independent action by the child threatens his attacker parents, spurring them to retaliate bitterly against the child. Consequently, he becomes strikingly sensitive to his parents' control. He attempts to break from his distasteful dependency by rebelling, denying his inadequacies and proving to the world that he is independent.

Dick Benton, for example, painfully remarked to me in a counseling session,

> My father is a mean S.O.B. He beat me so much I finally ran away when I was fifteen. Later I joined the Marines where I found a whole bunch of guys just like my dad. Jesus, I've spent my whole life running away from him.

It is striking to note that Dick's three teen-age children expressed almost identical feeling toward him. The eldest boy ran away from home and became a heavy drug user. The younger twin boys had

---

1. Interestingly, several studies have found that children raised by rejecting, indifferent, arbitrary, and domineering parents have high rates of juvenile delinquency and other forms of social deviancy in their ranks (O. J. Harvey, *Conceptual Systems and Personality Organization*, 1961, p. 296).

been kicked out of numerous schools, arrested for stealing a car, and were overtly hostile toward Dick and his wife.

With few stable guidelines to decide what to do to be a good person, the attacker becomes hopelessly frustrated. So, he gives up trying to improve or even to maintain his relations with his parents. He says to himself, "Okay, from now on we're at war! You hate me and I hate you! That's clear; let's fight!" Ambivalent feelings of both love and hate toward his parents, which are normal in most children, are eliminated. He says, "Whatever you do, I am going to do just the opposite! And furthermore, I'm going to get you back since you got me!"

You must remember, of course, that forces other than parents significantly mold a person's motivations. If you attend a school that is heavily dominated by attackers, you would most likely acquire attacker tendencies. If your peers, work associates, and boss are attackers, they would produce attacker needs in you. Parents are the original builders of your psychological needs; however, all of your encounters mold your personality. Consequently, subtle changes in motivation occur constantly as you change environments.

The Attacker Is Defiant

To prove his independence to the world, the attacker eagerly rebels against authority, social customs, and other accepted practices. He stubbornly opposes most directives, especially when someone tries to make him responsible, cooperative, or dependent. When you confront him with this fact, he denies it vehemently. Resisting feedback just as he opposes attempts at control, he rejects both you and the feedback. If he makes a mistake, is forced to take a stand or is openly criticized, he refuses cooperation from that moment on. He may reject the simplest request with harshness, quite out of proportion to the event, by releasing his tensions, offering excuses, articulating rationalizations, blaming others and becoming rigid[2] (Karen Horney, *Our Inner Conflicts*, 1945, p. 64).

2. Because power figures are so important to him, however, the attacker ends up being almost as dependent on them as is the avoider. The only difference is that the attacker does the opposite of what the authority wants. The avoider, of course, complies with those in control.

To oppose authorities the attacker might steal a car, become sexually promiscuous, or get arrested to prove his "independence." His rebellion might, on the other hand, take the form of more acceptable patterns of resistance. He might question authorities or subtly steer a group away from the leader to validate the fact that he is "free."

A fascinating illustration of socially-acceptable defiance was revealed by a bright lathe operator in a manufacturing plant. He constantly taunted his supervisor. Once he placed a notice on the bulletin board which critically demanded to know why management had not made certain tools available to workers. He quoted various technical authorities who highly recommended their use. After each quotation he inserted a penetrating challenge to his supervisor and the management. Following several of these occurrences and discussions with the worker, his supervisor passed a policy forbidding the posting of notices. The attacker took this as a personal challenge and constructed a private bulletin board next to his workbench and filled it with critical notices. Shortly thereafter, his supervisor called him in to discuss the matter. The attacker defiantly abused his boss, and told him to go to hell, which resulted in his being fired. Interestingly, this employee had a history of job-hopping, which is a common pattern for attackers. As he told the researcher, "I expected to be fired because it always happens. People have it in for me" (Abraham Zaleznik, *Human Dilemmas of Leadership*, 1966, p. 49).

Since he is difficult to get along with, people often reject the attacker. Then he says, "See, I told you I was right. People are basically no good." He makes a reality out of his fantasy. He creates a self-fulfilling prophesy by struggling with others, especially authority figures, and ultimately loses his struggles. He loses partly to escape authority and responsibility and partly to fulfill his fantasy about the evil nature of people.

One attacker leader, who managed his family's chain of high-class restaurants, decided to defy the firm's traditions by leading the company into lower income markets. This action shocked his upper-crust family so violently that they attempted to stop him. He fought their control by becoming more vigorous in his "lower-class expansion" program. He observed, "Those damn snobs! They've been trying to run things too long and this really gets them where it hurts! I have collected enough documented legal evidence to stop them. I sent them a letter telling them I am ready to meet in court at any time, with a full public hearing if we got into court.'' He continued by pointing out, ''All my friends are talking about me for dealing with lower-class people. They can't figure me out! Ha, ha!''

In a similar case, one attacker physician said, ''I teach my partners to charge high prices for our services. A lot of times a patient says, 'Isn't that pretty steep?' and I say, 'Yes!' Then the patient asks, 'Why do you charge so much?' I respond by saying 'Because I like to!' If you get into a discussion about your pricing, you just can't win. Patients raise hell with all kinds of stupid questions. It just isn't worth it!''

The attacker, then, is over-sensitive to power. As one teacher described a child, ''He wants to be the center of his world. whatever is wrong, Mother gets the blame . . . he tends to be extremely negative in his response to others. That he has been asked to do something is, in his eye, sufficient reason for refusing to do it'' (Harvey, et. al., p. 99).

The Attacker is Hostile

The attacker's punitive upbringing causes him to be antagonistic and nit-picking—his major aim is to be counterproductive. He turns the simplest events into wars. A great debater, he steers you off the main issues by forcing you to argue about inconsequential facts. You become so upset that the original goals of your discussion are lost in the confusion. This pleases him.

One speaker I know told a management conference on human relations, ''If you want to solve a conflict, just listen to the people and don't say a word. People are just like balloons. Let their air out and they relax. Get a balloon when you are mad and let your air out,'' he continued. The next day one of the managers, who was diagnosed by his peers as a pure attacker, blew up and let the air our of over two-hundred balloons in the classroom throughout the day. This attacker enjoyed ridiculing the group leader in a clever manner.

Adolf Hitler's constant barroom fights in his younger years and in political meetings in his later years, revealed a vicious, argumentative man who thrived on antagonism. Indeed, he became, unfortunately, a master of fighting.

Another attacker illustrated his debating ability in a small sales firm that had been trying to establish a performance review system. This is a method for evaluating employees' performance periodically and rewarding them according to their output. When the management finally gathered to decide on the matter, several hours of lively discussion occurred. An informal consensus evolved and the president said, "It looks like we are all pretty much behind this revised plan. Are there any final comments?" Everyone suddenly had the sinking feeling that there would be, and they all knew who would make them—Jack Anders, the attacker. Not too surprisingly, he raised his hand and said, "I don't see how you could think of putting something this poorly thought-out into operation. What does performance really mean? How can our men, with so little training, really give good counseling interviews? You are out to lunch!" The meeting broke into emotional debates. Minor points were illogically argued, and the proposal was finally sent back to committee for further study. One of the managers said afterward: "We were sick of the discussion, and we knew we couldn't win an argument with Jack. We just decided to go home and forget it." Jack, however, appeared to enjoy "having a good fight."

Mr. Morris, one of the English governors in the United States in the 1750s, was in my judgment, a good example of an attacker leader. As he described himself, "You know I love disputing; it is one of my greatest pleasures. . . ." But, Benjamin Franklin, an achiever, observed that "these confuting people like Mr. Morris are generally unfortunate in their affairs. They get victory sometimes, but they never get good will, which would be of more use to them in the long run" (p. 164).

Release pent-up anger comes from crushing others. When someone other than yourself is receiving his blows, his sarcasm appears witty. When his tart humor hits close to home, however, it is not funny. The attacker husband and wife team, for instance, often make others embarrassingly uncomfortable with their degrading assaults and bitter battles. I was struck by the mood which prevailed in a movie theater after a showing of Edward Albee's hostile play about family fighting, *Who's Afraid of Virginia Woolf?* The husband and wife had displayed an open viciousness which left the audience excited, curious, vicariously satisfied, yet shocked and frightened. This is how most people feel about the attacker.

This play also portrayed well the sadistic nature of the attacker's sense of humor. He relishes another's misfortunes and especially enjoys biting sarcasm and bold acts which defy proper customs and authorities. Obviously, he cannot be too open with his pleasure at another's pain. But if you observe carefully, you will perceive his delight in another's injury. When he can make another look inferior, he appears superior.

The attacker's bitterness comes out more under stress. If he makes a mistake at work, he lashes out at the first person he meets. If he hits a pressure drive into a lake while playing golf, he is apt to cut down his partner.

You might think of a famous comedian, for example, who has based his career on his degrading of others. Almost instantaneously he can rip someone apart, find the weaknesses that most people overlook and highlight them publicly. If you have a big nose, this is what he kids you about. If you are short, he asks you to step out of that hole in the ground. He mimics your voice, expressions, and mannerisms just enough to make you look awkward. He uses his humor to make you suffer as he has suffered, yet pretends that his sarcasm is all in jest.

Interestingly, the attacker often prefers to hurt those who are the nicest, most vulnerable individuals. He sees in the pleaser, for instance, the qualities he lacks; therefore, he wants to destroy them. The attacker believes that admitting weakness or even being nice is to acknowledge dependency, which he eagerly wants to avoid. So he lashes out at those whom he considers weak because they are a threat to his self-image. The flamboyant, boastful behavior of Harold in Kurt Vonnegut's play, *Happy Birthday, Wanda June*, illustrates the attacker's desperate need to hunt and kill in highly visible ways.

The case of Stan, a West Coast school superintendent, shows the importance for the attacker of performing his attacks publicly. To prove his independence, he must be seen disparaging authority. For others to be really hurt, they must know they have been stung. One of Stan's subordinates, Bill Hadden, a principal of one of the schools in Stan's district, had diligently worked on a reorganization plan for his community's school system. Stan came to Bill's home to review the proposal. They worked through dinner. Stan, an attacker, made repeated passes at Bill's wife during dinner. Bill and his wife ignored Stan's aggressions as best they could, but they suffered silently. Stan watched Bill carefully to measure his success in hurting Bill. Stan looked as if he were thoroughly enjoying Bill's pain. Finally, Stan said to Bill's wife, "Boy, if you don't stop walking back and forth out here, I'm going to grab that cute little bottom of yours." Shortly thereafter, Bill called the meeting to a close. Stan acted unaware that he had been callously harming his "friends." Possibly it was unconscious, but it was typical of his behavior both on and off the job.

Bill mentioned later that Stan was notorious for sleeping with women in every city he visited. He would go to conventions just to sexually conquer and exploit his female targets. In an interview with one of Stan's secretaries, she commented, "Well, you really have to watch him. He's always after you! Also, he sure yells a lot over the phone. It seems like he is always cussing somebody out for something."

One of Stan's principals commented, "There is nothing quite so unpleasant as to work with Stan. He'll call me at home any time of the night and raise all kinds of hell with me! He screams, often calling me vicious names. He almost demands that I do this and that, and keeps implying that he thinks everyone else here is stupid."

The attacker, then, is by nature cynical and negative. He sees the world as basically stupid and other people as rather worthless. One attacker described his teachers by saying they are:

> Miserable, . . . always mad . . . sneering . . . try to make you feel little, (and later) wouldn't get along with'em . . . wouldn't give you half a chance . . . they'd just jump down your neck.

In describing his peers he used the following:

> Always bothering you . . . give you a hard time . . . big shots . . . better than everybody . . . show off . . . bragging . . . shoving everyone around (and later) act like they are your friends at times but you know they aren't. (Harvey, et. al., p. 66)

Similarly, attacker students constantly twit their professors by coming in late, noisily shuffling, talking, or ridiculing their pet ideas. This is how they release their hostilities. These descriptions of how he sees others, clearly illustrate the negative filters through which the attacker perceives his world.

The Attacker Rejects Responsibilities

The attacker develops a large supply of creative talent to hide from responsibilities. He develops heightened sensitivity to control centers within a situation, then dodges the danger spots and cracks the weak joints.

He Acts Uncommitted One technique the attacker uses to defend himself from responsibilities is to act uncommitted. His apparent indifference is often an anticipatory ploy to beat others to the punch, since they cannot deprecate his abilities if he had no intention of performing an act in the first place. An example of this is the sour grapes fable where the fox pretended he *did not want* some grapes, when in fact he *could not reach* them. The attacker attributes failure to his lack of interest, not to his lack of skill.

In training programs, the attacker frequently demonstrates his lack of commitment by conspicuously showing disdain for those who participate. He carries on side conversations, pretending to be irritable and restless.

He Gives Variable Commitment A slight variation of the noncommitment ploy is the *variable commitment act*. In this case, the attacker changes quickly, jumps from one issue to another, and gives such confusion information about his preferences that it is impossible to pin him down and evaluate his behavior. By revealing contradictory intentions, he eludes observer's interpretations.

He Disrupts Another technique the attacker uses to remain uncommitted is to disrupt operations. He challenges procedures, and shows his displeasure at being involved with a group that is working to improve things. One such event occurred in a seminar in which the attacker sat quietly during the slow periods of the group's discussions. When things started to click, however, he tried to change the subject to derail the leader and to ridicule the other members for being involved. Apparently, he could not bear to see the others making progress.

Another attacker, who had just accepted the presidency of a university, made his acceptance speech to the board and senior faculty by stating, "Our university is a dying institution that is filled with professors who have lead in their bottoms and rust in their heads. Our campus is an ugly eye sore to everyone! We need drastic surgery! We'll have to do it my way or one or the other of us will depart!"

He Imputes Evil to Others   If the attacker is unable to deny his responsibility, he often turns to the technique of imputing evil to others. He comments, "They are just trying to give me a hard time." "They had it in for me." "They are crooked cheats." "They are selfish people." "He just wishes he were as good as I am." By placing the blame on others' evil intentions, he escapes dependency and rationalizes his expression of anger toward them.

In one case, a wealthy retailer received a speeding ticket for going forty-five miles an hour in a thirty-five mile zone. This attacker became so angry at the police for giving him a ticket for such a "minor violation" that, rather than pay the small fine, he went to court, pleaded innocent and defended himself. He did meticulous research, drove 260 miles round-trip to court and went back four times because of delayed trials, court overloads, and continuations. On the fifth occasion, the judge dismissed the case because it was such a bother. This attacker took great pride in retelling the story of how "The police and courts had it in for me, but I beat them."

Interestingly, several of his colleagues commented that he spent most of his time in minor projects like this low-priority undertaking and seldom worked on significant issues for his company.

He Makes Everything an Emergency   The attacker also skillfully defies responsibility by making everything an emergency. He comments, "Your assignment has to be done now! I need this request immediately or the whole company will fold!" If he can fluster you, you make mistakes and become more vulnerable while he rides the waves. By constantly interrupting and pushing, he is able to *hit and run*, to dominate without having to implement. He can change tactics easily since it is difficult to keep up with him under "emergency conditions."

He Finds Fault The attacker expends much energy researching the mistakes of others and expanding on them publicly. Finding fault and assigning blame to others is one of his major talents.

The marketing director for a flower shop chain was trying to get all his outlets to follow a specific new marketing strategy. To determine whether stores were conforming to his plans, this attacker sent "undercover employees" to observe operations. When he heard through the grapevine that one of his Oregon stores was not following his plan, he immediately assigned his best agent to fly to Portland to case the store. In order to get his man there quickly, he hired a private plane to fly him to Chicago. Then, because the man would be a few minutes late for a commercial connection from Chicago to Portland, he called the radio tower and told them, "There is a serious medical emergency. Please hold the plane just a few minutes for my man." They did so. The spy found that the store was a deviant. The attacker gave the president the information and urged him to "really set an example with this man. This attacker found a little mistake, blew it out of proportion, and then got others to levy injurious punishment. He was thrilled.

He Forms An Attack Squadron The attacker builds a team of supporters around him who are also attackers to shield him from responsibility. His attack squadron performs three functions. First, they support him in his fights with others by giving him ammunition to use, first-aid after a skirmish, and encouragement and renewed confidence for his next encounters. Second, the attack squadron provides a forum for venting his hostilities and relieving his tensions, for within "their group," they feel safe and relaxed because they know they can viciously abuse each other but still be accepted. Third, a squadron is a human arena where the attacker can hit and run at will. The team members try to dominate and rebel against each other rather than offer constructive ideas. The accepted practice among squadron members is to jump into the middle of things within the group, try to cause a revolution, and then disappear. Against outsiders, however, the squadron presents a solid front.

The squadron may be composed of loosely-knit members, joined only by phone conversations or infrequent meetings that are saved for emergencies when and attacker is under pressure. He then calls his fellow attackers for counsel but covers his needs, so he will not reveal his weaknesses, by saying, "I want to bring you up to date on what's happening." After the conversation, he renews his battle with added support: "My friend, who is the expert on this matter, said I was right."

In several companies, I have found attack squadrons in closely-knit groups. In a large chemical corporation, for instance, one of the first members of the personnel department I interviewed displayed classic attacker characteristics. He bitterly assaulted everyone in the company and told me how ineffective his own department was. Similar cynical perspectives were provided by five out of the other seven managers in his department. Although these men had all worked in different divisions, they slowly gravitated together. They were quite unhappy and gleefully tore each other and everything that moved apart. The other departments in the company readily attested to this state of affairs with story upon story of their conflicts, noncompletion of projects, degrading of others' efforts and poor implementation of assignments. The squadron members complained seriously for hours and asked me about job openings in other companies, yet they never really looked for another position. They seemed to prefer to remain in their misery.

The Attacker Seldom Admits He Is Wrong

The attacker, even more than the commander, seldom admits to others or himself that he is wrong. He denies negative feedback, pretends things came out better than they did, blames others for failures, and seldom, if ever, loses and argument. He believes you should never say you are sorry.

Similarly, the attacker hates to admit fear of any kind for he feels it indicates weakness. Consequently, he might make himself do things which he especially fears. If he is afraid of horses, he might ride the toughest of the bunch. If he is frightened of homosexual feelings, he might take especially masculine roles, hang around with tough guys, tell hard jokes, hug masculine men, and act unconcerned about doing so. These counterphobic acts allow him to deny his fears and display supposed strengths. His weaknesses are thus well disguised and kept under careful control.

Part of the reason the attacker does not admit he is wrong is that he devalues others; thus he seldom listens, hears, or accepts feedback about his performance, especially if it is negative. As one attacker phrased it, "Why should I listen to trash coming from a pile of rubbish?" By defensively ignoring signs of failure, the attacker often continues blindly in the face of disaster.

One subordinate said about his attacker president, "When he first came here a year ago, he told us all the heartbreaking tales of how people had taken advantage of him in St. Louis where he had worked before. Now after a year with him I can see why. And I'll bet you $100 that right now he is telling someone else how we all screwed him by quitting. He just does not admit to himself that he helps to cause his problems."

The Attacker Is Cold Interpersonally

The attacker's face reveals a somber composure, grave lines and severe eyes. He speaks and walks sternly. When you enter a room, he does not greet you cordially. Both his verbal and nonverbal gestures communicate hostility, which causes you to feel afraid and cool toward him.

Interestingly, one of Dick Benton's victims in the real estate development firm commented, "I left the company one year ago and haven't seen Benton since, and I hope I never do. Just the thought of the hostile, anguished look on his face makes me sick!"

Henry Miller poetically describes a friend of his who seems to me to be an attacker: "Jaime de Ongulo was unpredictable after . . . he had a few drinks under his belt. The occasions when he did visit us and leave without making a scene, without cursing, reviling, and insulting everyone, were few and far between," I cannot resist quoting another fine passage about Miller's "wild duck," "outlaw" friend: "It was shortly after lunch that Jaime rode up, hitched his horse to the oak tree, gave it a punch in the ribs, and descended the steps (Henry Miller, *Big Sur*, 1957, p. 345).

Genuine smiles or warm belly laughs seldom escape from the attackers for he is not at peace with himself. One college quarterback told the story about an attacker who played end for his team. After a play was finished, the attacker would walk back to the huddle slowly and defiantly. After a play was called, he would meander to the line of scrimmage. The quarterback would yell to him, "Come on, John, let's hustle!" As the quarterback put it,

I was always struck by the fact that he would really sneer at me
when I'd say that. He almost walked with his fists clenched as if her
were ready to hit me, despite the half smile on his face. When I
would pat him on the shoulder and say, "Come on let's go," he'd
stiffen so fast, he got like a statue. He just walked around like he
hated people and was always ready for a fight. In fact, he got into
a lot of them.

The lathe operator we discussed earlier in this chapter, who posted
notices in the plant and later by his workbench, ". . .lived a lonely
existence as a middle-aged bachelor with no friends. He enjoyed
one activity: chess competition. He was a gifted player, and this in
itself was revealing because it indicated that his main human relationships existed within a ritual of combat in the two-person relationship: victor and vanquished" (Zaleznik, p. 67).

One attacker who owned an insurance firm took great delight in
relating how his management controlled their employees:

> Our young guys who do well and begin to see that the company
> keeps a lot of the money they produce usually ask for raises. They
> threaten to quit and to go into business for themselves. My sales
> manager is really great. He says, "We pay you to do a good job for
> the company. If you don't like it, leave." Man, we had one guy
> who quit and told us over and over again that he wouldn't work for
> us again if it was the last thing he did. About three months later he
> came crawling back. His wife felt she had been deprived too long
> and bought a whole bunch of furniture for their house. He had to
> get cash quickly so he came back. Boy, was that great!

One attacker leader who worked for a chain of pizza restaurants
was faced with an investigation by his local Internal Revenue Service agent who happened to suffer from asthma. The attacker ush-
ered the agent into a small office which had no windows or air
conditioning. He turned up the heater and chain-smoked during the
meeting. Afterwards, the attacker laughingly told how the IRS agent
had coughed, wheezed, blinked his eyes and left in a hurry. As this
example illustrates, an attacker often defines his conflicts as "win-
lose" games. He approaches his problems, therefore, by assuming
that antagonism is already present, and that others are his enemies.

Since the attacker often asserts his wishes, gives orders, expresses
anger, defends himself and opposes suggestions, he appears unin-
hibited. Actually he is closed interpersonally, and lacks the ability

to relate in a positive manner. Accordingly, love is relatively un-important to him. He marries but sees little reason to be considerate, warm, or giving. He says, "Why should I worry? Let others take care of themselves." All feelings and emotions are viewed as "sloppy sentimentality."

For him, Toughness is greatness. But in acting out this belief he ". . .acts like the man who chased beggars from his door because they were breaking his heart" (Horney, p. 68). He fights his softer human feelings to bolster himself because considerate people reflect what he lacks. He refuses kindness and abuses it, but inwardly he has a vacuum of painful loneliness that he yearns to fill.

The external appearances of the attacker's lifestyle reflect his needs. His office, home, and style of dress, are unadorned, even grave. He seems to prefer the austere to the colorful, the stringent to the lively, for they prevent others from gaining insights about him by their lack of uniqueness. In fact, in observing the eating habits of attackers, I have noticed a startling preference for acidic, sour foods, drink, hot spices, vinegars and other bitter tasting foods. I have observed many attackers with streams of tears rolling down their red cheeks, exclaiming how they loved the red peppers they were eating.

The attacker often fails to perceive the difference in the com-munication he receives. He frequently cannot distinguish between positive and negative feedback or approval and disapproval. If a person gives him a genuine compliment, he takes it as a threatening remark, ignores it, or moves to the attack. When he is criticized, there is no question about his reaction—he fights. In a sense, he disregards the emotional content of the information he receives, thereby remaining uninvolved while venting hostility and avoiding having to reveal his true self.

A professor who ridicules his students when they ask honest questions, changes the subject arbitrarily and communicates his constant disdain for "these ignorant youth" portrays this frigid manner. Or, a coach who enjoys seeing his players suffer by ig-noring their injuries reflects the attacker's aloofness.

The Attacker Has an Aggressive Sexual Style

The attacker's sexual style reflects his abrasive manner. He prefers to conquer his mate, to dominate and hurt this person. He finds it thrilling to thrash around violently, to move aggressively and to invent novel, shocking techniques of making love. Typically, an attacker's spouse feels that he is insensitive, coercive, and selfish. One wife of an attacker remarked, "As long as he is satisfied, he couldn't care less about me. He thinks I don't have any feelings. When he's ready he says, 'Let's go!' If I say 'well, let's talk first, and go slowly, because I don't feel like it yet,' he gets furious. he even hits me sometimes. He takes it personally, like an attack on his manhood or something." The more unconventional the occasion, the more the attacker enjoys his sexual relations, for he views intercourse as a conquest over his partner and over social standards which he feels restrict his freedom.

The attacker derives special pleasure, then, from making love in unusual places and under strenuous condition. One rather bedraggled newly-married executive exclaimed in a counseling interview, "my wife wears out. She loves to bite me. I lose concentration on making love because she sticks her nails into my back till I feel like screaming, 'Stop it, damn it.' She just kind of goes wild, like she is trying to hurt me." This, of course, is what the attacker is trying to do.

The Attacker Performs Well in Independent Jobs

The attacker prefers jobs in which he does not have to depend on others or to take much personal responsibility. He sets moderate goals and takes few risks—somewhat lower risks than the commander takes. If he can acquire the proper training, he does well as a writer, musician, artist, scientist, or professor. A perfect occupation for him is that of a critic—a social, movie, book, or theater critic. Here he must see what others have done and then tear their work apart. You might think of a movie or social critic you see frequently on T.V. What type of facial expression does he have? What tone of voice and inflection does he use? The role of a critic allows an attacker to vent his anger, defy accepted traditions, hit and run and maintain his "pseudoindependence." Tough sales are also jobs in which the attacker frequently does very well. When they can be independent and aggressive, attackers excel.

Some professions are more suited to the critic's role than others. A field such as the social sciences, for instance, has as one of its major tasks, the study of social customs and traditions. It is a natural role in which the attacker can hide under an intellectual's shield. By no means, however, are most social scientists attackers, but the role is compatible.

Similarly, the role of a revolutionary is congenial for the attacker's operations. He can defy authority figures, bomb buildings, hit people, and injure others under the rationalization that he is working for a better society. Traditionally, of course, rebels are always asked the final question, "Okay, suppose you are right. What we're doing now is horrible. What is your alternative?" And many true attackers have not gotten that far yet. It is important to mention here that all rebels are not attackers. There are many achievers, pleasers, commanders, and others in their ranks. It just happens to be a congenial role for the attacker to operate in while covering his true needs.

Although he is constantly involved in stress and disagreements, the attacker often brings out overlooked points, conflicts, and potential weaknesses. His ideas can be helpful, regardless of his intentions. Accordingly, people often have difficulty deciding, "Is this guy really smart and constructive, or is he just cynical?" Similarly, since the attacker plans for future events so he can protect himself, he alerts others to potential problems in their operations. His complaints often provide helpful insights to key issues.

Hector Walker, a middle-manager for a large retail company, for example, used the training he had acquired in his army reserve courses in the secret service to collect potentially damaging information about his company. One year, at the firm's annual banquet, he got drunk, walked up onto the speakers' platform before several thousand employees and their wives, and publicly blasted many of the top managers of the company. Hector stood nose to nose with the president at the head table and, over the microphone, told him how incompetent he was. Silence gripped the large audience. After several repeated attacks on different members of top brass in the room, he loudly proclaimed, "And, if you try to fire me you had better think twice, because I've got enough evidence to blow this company apart. The government and competition would both pay me a bundle for this information."

The company did not fire this attacker for the management was indeed intimidated because they had long known of his penchant for secrecy and viciousness. They did not want Hector in the company, but were afraid to get rid of him. As a result, Hector was shifted around continuously from job to job.

Almost all large organizations have a division which is called the dumping ground for poor employees. Ineffective producers are gradually shifted to these organizational cemeteries. On several assignments which called for meticulous, critical reviews of present operations and cleaning out these dumping grounds, Hector had done a superlative job. He was an excellent hatchet man. He could fire people with glee. The company had to be careful, however, to withdraw him from his assaults before he completely buried the organization he was cleaning up.

Most managers were afraid of Hector because he would not play politics or keep quiet. He revealed weaknesses as he saw them. Many times Hector was right, but he seldom took enough responsibility to push his ideas into implementation. Strangely enough, he often kept the company alert, alive, and careful because of his constant picking, but he left a trail of hard feelings behind him. One of his colleagues commented, "You have to know Hector. He will fight anything that stands up, but down deep he is okay. You just have to ignore him or he'll get you entangled in a fight and no work will get done."

The Attacker Has Poor Psychological Health

The attacker's insides continually rumble with feelings of stress, persecution, and fear. He feels others have disdain for him, yet after he releases aggression toward them, he is choked by guilt for hurting others. He cannot help but crush those around him. Caught in this web, the attacker's private view of himself becomes more negative even though he presents a positive, strong face publicly. This artificiality further intensifies his anxiety. He experiences little joy in his everyday affairs, since he views life cynically. These conclusions cause me to rank him as having only 25 percent psychological health out of a possible 100 percent. This, of course, is simply a relative rank to compare the attacker to others. The attacker's positive points often reveal him to be witty and cleverly sarcastic. He perceives the irony in common occurrences that most of us miss. At times he is charming and entertaining, for he causes unusual breaks in routines. Even thought his self-esteem is low, he does not lay down, give or let others run over him easily. He makes an effort to control his own destiny. When I have pointed out the characteristic weaknesses to attackers, I have found they exert mod-

est effort to examine my observations and seek to improve in a
silent, unobtrusive manner if they are given support.

SUMMARY

You might look back at your original scores of the ten friends you
ranked at the end of chapter 1. Who on your list has the highest
need to attack? Can you think of someone you know in addition to
those on your list who has a dominant need to attack? How do you
feel about him? Does the preceding analysis fit him? How much of
this need do you have?

You will also find it most helpful if you will summarize, without
looking back, the nine major characteristics of attackers.

1. How was the attacker raised?

2. Why and how is he defiant?

3. Why is he hostile?

4. Why does he reject responsibilities?

5. Why does he form an attack squadron?

6. Why does he not admit he is wrong?

7. Why is he cold interpersonally?

8. How does he perform in independent jobs?

9. How psychologically healthy is the attacker?

CHAPTER 4

The Avoider

Judy often remarked, ''I have to have my three cups of coffee in the morning or I can't function.'' When she finished her coffee quota, Judy ritualistically settled into charting her astrology readings. Promptly at 12:15 she prepared her lunch, then retired to the couch to watch her favorite soap operas from 1:00 til 4:00. Dinner was routinely prepared, cocktails downed, and Judy gave the final evening hours to her TV. Her husband dozed nearby. On Tuesdays and Thursdays, Judy went shopping. Fridays were devoted to her hairdresser. This schedule was her life.

During a counseling session, Judy's husband remarked to me, ''She doesn't do anything. She hates to phone anyone, to drive anywhere or to join any group activities. She's kind of like an adult baby. I mean, I have to take care of her.''

Judy dressed neatly. She stood with shoulders dipped forward. Her neck was shortened by a lifetime of pulling her head into her body. Reflecting on this fact in a counseling session with me, Judy remarked, ''When I was little, I thought my breasts were too big, so I leaned forward to hide them.'' Judy's eyes seldom were raised, and the lines on her face drew an image of fear for those whom she encountered.

Judy was an avoider.

Who do you know that is most like Judy? Write his initials here. _____ What is his life style? _____

What kinds of activities does he enjoy? *Cheer Leading could*

How willing is he to take risks? *not*
What does he do in his spare time? *Sleep*
How do you feel about him? *I Love her but feel she's saved of* *taken advantage of*

One of Lincoln's first generals in the Civil War, McClellan, was in my judgment, an avoider. He procrastinated. He constantly shied away from tough battles complaining about the lack of supplies, men, and poor weather. He could not face tough assignments or take action. He believed that when you were in charge, you should ponder. When in trouble, delegate. When in doubt, mumble. Then refer the whole problem to a committee.

What kind of military leader would the person you thought of make? How successful would he be? How fulfilled is he? To answer these questions, it is helpful to understand how the avoider got to be as he is.

The Avoider Is Raised in a Fearful and Overprotected Environment

Parents mold their child into an avoider by worrying about his failures. The avoider's parents, typically avoiders themselves, are shy and evasive. Consequently, they shield themselves and their child from risks and responsibilities. They constantly remind him that he is weak, that there is something wrong with him, that he is inferior, and that he is likely to fail.

Although a child is given much apparent latitude to do what he wants because his parents overindulge him, when a child initiates an action, his parents say, "It's okay if you want to do it, but you might get run over by a car, get smashed, and have tire tracks across your bloody face." The parents actually do not structure what the child should do, but they react negatively when the child initiates action. They indirectly tell him what he should not do. The child is given what appears to be independence, but in reality, he is inhibited by his parents' signals of fear and pessimism.[1]

1. See, for a different perspective on this issue, an article by Teevan and Churchman in *Journal of Personality and Social Psychology*, 21, no. 3 (March 1972): 345–49.

Avoider parents evade acknowledging their child's mistakes and weaknesses. They do not let their child renew his efforts at achievement, and they prevent him from disappointment by taking elaborate precautions to protect him from failing. The child is seldom given the chance to rely on his own skills or to experience success or failure. Because of these influences, the child begins to see himself as inferior. He reasons, "Since my parents think I will fail, I must not be any good, so I had better watch myself or I'll get hurt."

Since avoider parents do not think much of themselves, they have quite low expectations for their child's performance. As one mother commented "My child shouldn't expect too much. After all, we never really got very far. We're just not that way. You just have to learn to stay in your place and get along."

Similar repressive forces from peers, school, work and other family members can produce styles of training identical to those of the avoider's parents. A boss, for example, who constantly communicates that he thinks you are inferior, lowers your self-confidence. Many members of minority groups know these feelings well from being labeled inferior human beings. They learn they are of little value; therefore, they had better hide. Robert Coles paints this process clearly for many migrant-worker children. They are trained to feel they are nobody, so they act accordingly (*Uprooted Children*, 1970).

The Avoider Has Low Self-Confidence

Self-confidence is a central foundation of personality since it affects most other dimensions of a person—his willingness to take risks, to explore, to receive, and to give feedback. A person with low self-confidence like the avoider is pessimistic and negative in these dimensions.

One avoider wrote the following story about the picture in chapter 1 of a group of people sitting around a conference table:

> The boss has just told the men that their report was horrible. They kind of knew it was going to end up that way. The man standing is saying it wasn't his fault because they were the ones who decided what to do. The group feels that the best thing to do is to just forget

the report, because they would probably screw it up again. Let someone else have a turn. You just can't win.

It is easy to see that this avoider projects his low self-confidence into the picture story. He feels he is unworthy.

An avoider, then, generally has little capacity to accept shame or humiliation. Since he is upset easily, he is careful to protect himself from getting hurt. Consequently, he is quite negative, controlled and cautious.

The director of an art museum, for example, was noted for speaking quietly. People often remarked that it was difficult to hear him. After several counseling sessions I mentioned this to the director. He commented, "I often am not confident in what I am saying, and so if I say it quietly, people will not be sure if they heard me accurately."

A graduate student in one of my classes, who had little self-confidence, exerted enormous effort to protect himself from being ridiculed as an inferior person. During his several years in graduate school he developed a reputation as a "party boy." He gave the impression that he never studied, drank all the time, and chased girls. Toward the end of his studies, he reported in an open, sensitivity-group discussion, however, that he would, in fact, pretend to be going out on a date but then sneak down to the university library and hide in the stacks to study. When the library closed, he would stop by the local pub for a beer and stagger into his apartment bragging of his conquests. He commented, "I couldn't stand for my friends to know that I actually was trying as hard as I could because I didn't see how I could face them if I didn't pass." Even though he got average grades, he could not have accepted the shame of failure if everyone knew he had tried, for then failing would have been *his* fault, not the fault of parties, beer, and girls.

This same attempt to protect against failure is illustrated frequently in other activities, because the avoider's low self-esteem causes him to take many detours around reality. Avoiders are nervous when competing in ego-involving tasks. The avoider who has a tennis match with a tough opponent will show up for the match with torn shoes, a slightly broken racket or some other "protective device." Or, the avoider golfer in the middle of a big match going to the eighteenth hole with the bets multiplying, hints about how his shoulder is killing him, or how he drank too much last night, and how his "hangover" is torture for him.

The Avoider Takes Few Risks

Because of his shaky self-esteem the avoider takes few risks. Since he has a low capacity to accept shame or humiliation, he cannot stand to make mistakes for they make him visible. When he must choose among alternatives, he takes the safest course.

While playing darts, for example, if he is allowed to stand as far from the board as he likes, the avoider walks right up and sticks the darts in the board. He thoroughly enjoys throwing darts from a short distance because this minimizes risks of failing.

Although he takes low *personal* risks, at times the avoider chooses assignments that are *objectively* very risky. In the dart game, if it is acknowledged by others that it is impossible to hit the bull's eye when he stands far from the board, he sometimes stands so far away that he can barely see it. When he fails, people say, "No one could have made it from that distance. It wasn't his fault."

A boss might say to his subordinate, for example, "John, we have an extremely difficult assignment here which we don't think anyone can accomplish. We want you to give it a try though, just to experiment with it." If John is an avoider, he is likely to say, "Great, I'd love to." Naturally, if he does not accomplish the assignment, John's co-workers and boss will feel, "Oh, that wasn't John's fault. No one could have succeeded at that task for it was impossible." Therefore, John has not failed, because he has taken a very difficult, risky task, but one that was for him a "low personal risk assignment."

If by chance the avoider actually succeeds on a risky assignment, it makes him unhappy, for this raises others' expectations for his performance in the future. He fears he will be pressured into more risky, responsible assignments. Thus, an avoider often fails on purpose just to lower others' expectations of his performance. The avoider feels that any success he has is due to luck or other external factors and that he will probably fail next time so he might as well do it now to prevent more serious problems in the future.

Henry Miller has described in detail a man who, in my opinion, is a classic avoider—Moricand. Miller portrays Moricand, the European intellectual, as "neat, orderly, immaculate, fussy, cautious. . .." Moricand's life was somber, fearful, always full of talk but lacking in action: "A fatalistic quality pervaded his whole being" (Miller, p. 275).

The Avoider Procrastinates

Because the avoider shies from risks, he has trouble making decisions. As one manager said of an avoider, "When he has a problem, he gathers reams of data, and really digs for it. He never quits, but there are no results. He comes to me and says, 'Well, the answer is in here somewhere.' But he won't commit himself for anything."

Another administrator of a federal agency in Washington commented in this regard about one of his employees: "Whenever he has a big problem, he delegates it and works on minor ones. He almost seems to say, 'If I don't bother to make a decision, I might not have to.' He will not do an extra assignment unless he is forced to."

In the 1750s an English general, Lord Loudoun, attempted to facilitate smooth relationships between England and the colonies. He appeared, in my judgment, to be an avoider. He delayed negotiations; he told travelers that ships were leaving for England, then delayed them for months. He agreed to pay certain debts, then did not face up to his obligations. As Ben Franklin so well phrased it, ". . . I wonder'd much how such a man came to be entrusted with so important a business as the conduct of a great army; but, having since seen more of the great world, and the means of obtaining, and the motives for giving places, my wonder is diminished" (Franklin, p. 148.)

In one incident, Franklin was to be reimbursed by Lord Loudoun for certain expenses. Lord Loudoun repeatedly delayed, excused, and skirted payment. Finally, just before Franklin was to sail for England, Loudoun sent him a message saying that, since he did not want to confuse things, he had placed Franklin's money in a letter to him which he could pick up on the ship after it sailed. Of course, when Franklin tried to find his letter, there was none. Lord Loudoun had chosen an escape from a difficult dilemma in such a way that he did not have to face the consequences. (Franklin, p. 148.)

The Avoider Is Dependent

Since the avoider does not want to fail, he depends on others. If he took responsibility for the outcomes of the things he worked on, he would expose himself to the possibility of failure, risk and visibility. So what he enjoys the most is to be *other-reliant*.

The avoider is not concerned much about what he does, as long as others decide for him and take the responsibility. Accordingly, the avoider prefers activities which (1) are governed by detailed guidelines, (2) contain few unexpected events, and (3) are repetitive. These situations allow him to depend on external factors rather than on himself.

The avoider housewife, for example, demonstrates her other-dependence in small ways. She asks her husband or children to make phone calls for her. She lets her friends decide where to go for lunch. She encourages her children to guide her life, and when asked her opinion, she says, "I don't care, you decide."

Because the avoider desires other-dependence, he works to collect status symbols to use to attract others. (His efforts to do so, however, are minor compared to the performer's.) Bill, an avoider, who was the accountant for a small textile company, anxiously sought a big title and was sensitive when someone else got a new carpet in his office or some other status symbol. When the company's top management was about to print their annual report, Bill ran into the president in the hall and said, "I hear my picture might not be included in the annual report. Is this true?" It really should not have been included, but the president said to himself, "Bill will give us so much grief if we don't; let's just go ahead and put it in."

In another case, Bob, an achiever, had a rush project with a critical deadline for delivering a report. His secretary could not find anyone to help her, so Bob pitched in. Bob's avoider boss, Derek, walked by and saw Bob up on a table assembling and stapling the report. Derek said, "Bob, we don't do things like that around here. What would other managers think if they saw you behaving like that?" This example points out the avoider's concern for propriety. As long as he stays respectable, people will have no reason to hurt him, and thus he can stay hidden.

The Avoider is a Non-explorer

The avoider, even more than a commander, is a non-experimenter. When faced with a problem, he does not think of trying out new ideas or changing his behavior. Because of his fatalistic approach to life, he maintains a way of doing a job long after it has proved ineffectual.

A couple of years ago I started playing tennis with another man, who was also a novice. For several months we were equal. Gradually, I started to beat him regularly and became bored with the matches. Out of curiosity, one afternoon after three sets of tennis, we sat down, had a Coke; and I asked him, "John, just for fun, how many first serves did you get in today?" John looked puzzled, scratched his head and said, "Gee, I don't know. Why do you ask?" I had counted, and he had gotten only three of his first serves during the entire afternoon. I later said, "Boy, those guys next to us were superb players, weren't they?" He replied, "I didn't notice them."

I also observed that John had not changed any aspect of his game during the two months we had been playing. He still served without looking at the net. He did not try to hold the racket differently or experiment with the way he threw the ball. Although John expressed the desire to play well, he had never experimented with ways to improve, such as taking lessons, practicing or observing the playing styles of others. Furthermore, he would very much have disliked my pointing these observations out to him or my efforts to "help" him improve.

Another illustration of the avoider's desire not to explore is his negative attitude toward training. He is highly opposed to training programs which focus on personality, communication, or leadership improvement, for these experiences prevent him from hiding. And, typically, those who need training the most are least interested in it. Those who have the weakest skills in managing others resist training the most.

The avoider wants to prevent variety in his life, so he sticks to routines. His preference for stability over variety causes him to spend a lot of his time thinking about the past rather than the future. He recalls the safe, pleasant, stable occurrences and ignores the risky and new. Since the status quo is very important to him, social changes like school integration and youth revolts are very threatening because his traditional safe guidelines for living are challenged. The answer to these threats for the avoider is to withdraw, not to explore.

The Avoider's Sexual Style

A cautious lover, the avoider freezes at the thought of intimacy. To make love by totally giving of himself in a relationship is as foreign to the avoider as is being spontaneous and open. To protect himself from the risks of failing to please his partner, of being rejected, hurt or ridiculed in his sexual encounter, the avoider mechanizes his sexual relationships. He is a cold lover and an aloof companion. Frigidity is his constant companion.

Sandra, a forty-year-old avoider, when struck by the urge for sexual intercourse, would casually, almost yawningly, remark to her husband, "Well, do you want to have sex tonight?" Sandra's husband, also an avoider, replied, "Well, I guess so." These partners revealed to me in counseling that they had intercourse about once every five weeks. They very seldom touched each other, never hugged, kissed, or showed physical affection. To naturally grab the other's hand, to touch the other's hair, or to rub the other's shoulder was unheard of for Sandra and her husband. Sexual contact was ugly and dirty to them as it is to most avoiders. Nakedness completely contradicts their need to hide.

The Avoider Does Not Like Feedback

Because his esteem is so fragile, the avoider dislikes feedback about his behavior. If you give a lot of positive feedback about his success on a job, the avoider denies it, points out all of his mistakes, and tries to convince you how poor the project actually was. He always expects the worst to happen, so if it does, he is not disappointed. He expends much energy reducing his image in your eyes. He wants to lower your expectations of his *performance* so that he cannot fail for you in the future. He wants status and respectability but does not want to earn it.

One avoider, the receptionist for an officer of a large automobile manufacturing firm, has a favorite comment: "You can't win." And not too surprisingly, she can't, because even when she wins, she perceives it as lucky and temporary. She says, "I know this can't happen again." Or, "Well, this is just temporary. I know things are going bad tomorrow. I always lose. It is just a matter of when." Whatever positive feedback the avoider receives, then, is clouded by pessimism.

The Avoider Performs Well in Easy Jobs

The avoider does a good job on tasks that are repetitive, easily mastered, constant, and governed by rules and procedures. When not required to learn or to improve with each successive task, he does well. Jobs such as key-punch operator, production worker, "traditional housewife" chores, (excluding child rearing), typist, or bookkeeper are suitable for an avoider, for he can continually do the same task without having to learn new skills or having to take new risks.

When the probability of being personally successful is high, the avoider does well. At school, for example, he prefers heterogeneous classes rather than having every one of the same ability together, because the mixed classes allow him to hide more easily. The avoider's ability to learn a job is also related to his success or failure. If he is given an easy job and then told he has done poorly, his continued learning is impaired. By contrast, when told he succeeded on an *easy* task, he learns faster than the achiever does on these easy tasks. If the avoider feels relaxed by the cooperative mood of the assignment, he does much better than when told, "This is a critical sales call," or "You have to do well on this exam."

College students, for instance, who are avoiders do worse than achievers in school. They also select easier majors and drop out of school four times as often as nonavoiders. In addition, avoiders prefer jobs and hobbies as adults which are cooperative rather than competitive, vague rather than concrete, for these activities have no clear possibilities for success or failure (John W. Atkinson, *An Introduction to Motivation*, 1964).

When the avoider is placed in an ego-involving, challenging pursuit, he sweats excessively, displays awkward movements, and laughs inappropriately. His performance is inhibited by his overwhelming fear of losing face. In sports, the favorite term for this familiar feeling is "choking." Anyone who has played a competitive sport understands the normal physical sensations of tightening-up, shaking, and having difficulty breathing which occur before the big game. The avoider feels this way all day long.

Dan was a leading golfer in his local country club, playing excellent golf until he faced pressure. Before the finals of a big match, in a counseling session, I asked Dan, "What would be the very worst thing that could happen to you tomorrow?" After much thinking he replied, "Let's see. I could lose ten down with eight holes to go, shoot a ninety-five, three-put every green, and have my wife, children, and friends follow me and laugh at me while I am screwing up." I then asked Dan how badly he would feel if he did the worst he could. He reflected and said, "You know, it would kind of be ridiculous, almost funny." I encouraged Dan to think through and face the actual consequence of failing. Facing failure enabled him to realize that it was not as horrible as he imagined it to be. This process often helps avoiders. It seemed to help Dan for he shot a low score the next day.

The results of the avoider's performance should not be confused with is efforts. Often the avoider will work as long, if not longer, than other employees. Rather than act upon a problem, however, if he is faced with a decision, he procrastinates. One Army administrator described an avoider this way:

> He puts in a phenomenal number of hours, but he never does anything. He'd spend the first two hours of the day planning his day, making rough drafts of his plans, and so forth. And we'd have to do the same thing. He'd make us plan our day for hours. Also, he'd often come in at the end of the day with a big rush project we had to get out. But it was usually an insignificant assignment.

Another manager described his avoider subordinate like this:

> If he is given a task with careful instructions to follow, he will perform it well. If he is through with his work for the day by 3:00 in the afternoon, he will sit in his office and worry about his work, rather than initiate new projects, go home, or talk with people.

One banker observed:

> We have a teller in the bank who would just sit at his desk all day

and fret if someone didn't tell him what to do. If his replacement for lunch did not come on time he raised hell. He'd call upstairs and really fuss. Every job had to be done precisely. If it wasn't, he'd get real nervous and wouldn't do it. If he failed at it, he always had a thousand excuses. As long as there were definite assignments, however, he was a perfectionist at following the rules and carrying out instructions. He was a stickler for detail, for this defined the minimal level of acceptable behavior for him.

Thus the avoider performs best in clearly-defined jobs where others direct his behavior, or the rules define what he should do.

An Avoider Has Poor Psychological Health

As the previous discussion illustrates, the avoider has very poor psychological health. His view of himself is pasted together with negative, sorrowful concepts. Indeed, his deep, frequent sighs symbolize his downfallen self-image. He is, in fact, so fragile, shallow, and tender that he withdraws from life hoping to escape from further suffering, rather than moving toward growth or enrichment. His life's goal is to hide. When he is ready to die, he hopes he can say, "Ah, I made it. No one saw me, heard me, or exposed me. I escaped without being noticed."

Life is a difficult chore, a painful experience for the avoider. Withdrawal is his safest route to shield himself from the suffering he expects. Accordingly, his high state of anxiety reveals his deep inner tension. He communicates these indicators of stress like neon signs by the strains on his face, the tightness of his mouth and the fidgeting in his eyes. A direct question or request for his opinion is enough to turn his face flush red and his movements into jerky seizures, for he believes his answers will be significantly inferior. In my judgment, these characteristics indicate that avoiders are very unhealthy psychologically—I give them the lowest score, 15 out of a possible 100 on psychological health. This score merely indicates my relative ranking of avoiders' degree of fulfillment, not an absolute measure. (I might mention a hunch I have observed, although unsystematically, that avoiders have a significant frequency of ulcers, hypertension and other similarly-related physiological illnesses that seem to match their psychological state. Also, they appear to have high rates of alcoholism and drug addiction.)

An avoider's strengths are that he is relatively easy to control and thus easy to get along with. He follows instructions carefully, seldom creates conflicts or openly criticizes. Since he understands more poignantly than others what it means to be unfulfilled, he is sensitive to the weaknesses and sufferings in others. Consequently, he is often kind and gentle, giving comfort to those in trouble.

SUMMARY

Each of us has some avoider needs, but some individuals need to avoid failure so much that this motivation dominates their lives.

How well does the analysis presented here fit the avoiders you know? Can you understand more clearly why your avoider friends behave as they do? How can you relate to them to develop a more satisfactory association? Do you want to? How would you help them change if they asked you to assist them?

For your summary, please see how many of the avoider's main characteristics you can recall. By recalling your own thoughts, your ability to internalize the significant motivational dimensions of avoiders should be enhanced.

1. Dependent

2. Takes few Risks

3. Low self confidence

4. Does not Like feedback

5. Non-explorer

6. Procrastinates

7. Poor Phys. health

8.

9. Does well is easy Jobs

10.

CHAPTER 5

The Pleaser

Dave, the personnel manager for an insurance firm, smiled easily and was on a first-name basis with many people. His plump body gave him a soft appearance. He rolled when he walked and seldom raised his voice.

"I don't care, it's up to you. Honestly, it doesn't make any difference to me." Dave's friendly words were his trademark, for he said them so frequently that they had become automatic reflexes. He talked with the employees in his firm when they had problems, listened well, supported sympathetically their dilemmas. Yet, Dave's boss said to me:

> I just don't know what I'm going to do with Dave. He's nice. Everybody likes him, but he's not doing the job. I asked him eight months ago to finish the job descriptions for three departments. He keeps telling me he's busy. He kind of keeps everyone in the company glued together. He's like honey. But he's all sweet and no sweat. I finally sat down with him and laid it on the line. I told him to finish the four projects I have him or else he was in serious trouble. He hasn't done them yet, and he doesn't seem to be worried. What can I do?

Dave, a pleaser, was finally transferred to a lower-level staff job where he happily continued in his pleaser life style.

Who do you know that is most similar to Dave? Write in his initials here. ⎯⎯⎯⎯ Why does he behave this way?

_____ What things does he do best? _____
How genuinely happy do you think he is? _____
How do you like him? _____

The pleaser you thought of probably craves acceptance and approval; thus, he is nice to almost everyone in hopes they will like him.[1] In a conversation, the pleaser selects those elements which refer to people, relationships, and positive feelings rather than performance. If, however, his peer group happens to be working hard, he will be happy to go along with them to feel accepted.

One pleaser housewife wrote the following story about the picture in chapter 1 of a group of individuals sitting around the table:

> These people are talking about the community Fourth of July celebration coming up next week. This is a chance for everyone to join hand-in-hand to draw all of the families together. They have enjoyed working together as a group to plan the celebration. Now they will have fun at the occasion.

The pleaser likes to make others happy. He is kind, generous, thoughtful, and considerate. President William Howard Taft's smiling ways, for example, certainly suggest that the pleaser need was one of his primary motivations.

The pleaser is often confused with the avoider because they both lack self-reliance, but they demonstrate it in different forms. The avoider, for instance, is shy and retiring, while the pleaser is outgoing and sociable. The pleaser loses his individuality by getting actively involved in groups; the avoider hides his identity by keeping to himself.

---

1. Past research has referred to the need to please as the need for affiliation. However, much of this research has seriously confused the affiliation or pleaser need with the avoider need. Thus, to prevent confusion, I thought it best to use separate terms. Also, the need to please captures the essence of this personality type more than does the need to affiliate, because affiliating, or spending time with others, is the means to the end of pleasing, and not the ultimate goal of making people happy. A pleaser is significantly motivated to actively please people in order to gain acceptance. For example, it may be that in his particular reference group he gains the most approval or acceptance by isolating himself from others for long periods of time. Therefore, he would have little affiliation, but he would please others and gain the approval he so badly needs. See for example Stanley Schacter, *The Psychology of Affiliation*, 1959.

The Pleaser's Training Environment Is Overcaring

The pleaser is trained by parents (or teachers, bosses, etc.) who are warm, loving, and overprotective. His parents do not encourage him to become excellent in any hobby or skill other than pleasing people. Since the parents themselves are pleasers, they go to extremes to free the child from conflict, pain, and suffering.[2]

If her five-year-old, for example, was not invited to a friend's birthday party, the pleaser-mother might drop by to visit the party-giver's mother hoping that this would get her daughter invited, thus freeing her from unhappiness.

Pleaser parents seldom argue in front of their children. They smooth over conflicts, joke, and have fun with each other, for they are themselves pleasers. Primarily, they teach their child to live for the present and to seek friendships. If the child fails at an activity, the parents reassure him: ''We would rather have you at home with us anyhow than playing that rough game of football.''

If the child can be made to feel warm and comfortable, the pleaser parents feel they have done a good job. ''Son,'' they say, ''we may not have as many material things as some, but we are really happy and have a lot of close friends. This is what is most important.'' Consequently, the child grows up feeling relatively comfortable, happy, and tension-free, yet seldom taking self-responsibility. Unconsciously, he learns to gauge the feelings of others to ensure that they will react favorably to him as his parents do.

The Pleaser Needs to Be Accepted

Desiring relationships that are free of conflicts, the pleaser works to make you like him. His strong need for acceptance, however, causes some people to feel he is clinging and demanding. One automobile dealer said, ''My son-in-law always seeks my approval. Every chance he gets he almost begs for compliments and support. He seems to exert all of his energies just to be included in things

---

2. The paternalistic or kind commander is most likely a product of one commander parent and one pleaser parent.

even if he doesn't like them. I guess he really needs reassurance
or something.''

Another executive stated, ''My wife is really a pleaser. She
doesn't strive for anything in particular except being tranquilized
and having people over all the time. She relishes her friends and
family. If she didn't have those close ties, I don't know what she
would do. Whenever the kids fight, she dies.''

Even the dreams of pleasers stress efforts to smooth out problems
so friendships can grow. The underlying motivation of the pleaser
is to give so much that he gets all of his friends indebted to him.
He does so many favors that it is impossible to keep up with him
by returning as many nice gestures. He refuses others' efforts at
reciprocity so he can build up ''savings accounts'' that he can call
on when he is in need of support. By creating guilt in his associates,
he buys kindness from them.

The Pleaser Is Other-Directed

The pleaser is not a self-reliant person. He participates, but he does
not want to lead or to stand alone. What little initiative he takes is
to get involved with others, to find out what is going on, and to
discuss others' problems. By mastering jokes and clever conversations, he entices others to be with him and to protect him. He
spends an enormous amount of time with people telling them about
his personal feelings and attitudes. Frequently, he confesses some
of his weaknesses so others will understand him or why he is not
performing well. He believes that the more he is understood, the
more difficult it will be for people to reject him.

When a new decision must be made, however, the pleaser fades
into the background. When placed in a situation where he must
exert responsibility, the pleaser finds it difficult to rely on his skills.
His natural response is to talk with members of his group about the
situation, so they will give him direction and reassurance, to relieve
him of his responsibilities. He is group-reliant rather than self-
reliant.

Believing people are basically good, the pleaser concentrates on
people's strengths and ignores their weaknesses. If someone attacks
him, he smooths it over and keeps away from them, doing so
because of his intuitive sense which guides him away from offending

others. He is likely to have a sign on his wall which states, "If you can't say something nice, don't say anything at all."

One executive in a large government agency commented about a pleaser employee:

> In our administrative team, he doesn't seem to strive for any goal in particular. He is reasonable and willing to consider almost anything you suggest. He has a subtle, imperceptible manner of getting close to you so that you end up really wanting to help the guy. And you know I never thought of it until now, but, I do a whole bunch of his work for him without realizing it. He is such a nice guy that I just kind of evolve into taking over for him. He's still there talking and working with me, but I am taking most of the responsibility and initiative. I didn't even realize it, though, until I started to describe him to you.

This comment illustrates that the pleaser frequently catches his peers and superiors off guard. In fact, there is a good possibility that if you have the pleaser in your work group, you might be carrying a lot of his load without being aware of it. More importantly, you really do not mind because you like the pleaser and you are happy to help him. One high school basketball coach in the tough New York league commented, "If I were really honest with you, Gerald, I would have to say that I feel at times that my assistant coach, who is a pleaser, is too ingratiating, too nice and this makes me uncomfortable. But I still try to be helpful to him."

The Pleaser Is Highly Persuadable

His mind can be changed relatively easily and quickly, for the pleaser sways with the popular opinions. At a Board of Directors' meeting of the Green Ecology Corporation, one of the members who was a pleaser stated what he thought was a very popular idea: "I really think we should seek new financing through a stock issue." As he spoke, other directors shuffled, moaned, and indicated strong disagreement. Almost without stopping for a breath, the speaker continued, "But I don't feel too strongly about this point." The others laughed, rather kiddingly, as if they were saying, "Come on! Who are you kidding?"

The pleaser has a hard time saying no. Whenever he is asked to serve on a committee such as the Community Chest, Heart Fund, and *ad hoc* marketing study group or the Country Club Board, he can be persuaded to accept, especially if the appeal is to his friendship. He says yes because he does not want to hurt anyone's feelings, it gives him opportunities to be with people. It is easy for him to accept, furthermore, when he takes little initiative in carrying out the obligations he accepts.

The Pleaser's Sexual Style

The pleaser gives of himself readily in making love, but the giving is more superficial than real. The pleaser is a passive lover. He is more likely to lie quietly and be made love to, than to initiate, experiment, explore, manipulate, or otherwise exert aggressive, passionate acts. Erogenous zones of his partner may be held but not caressed by the pleaser.

He is a touching, hugging, feeling partner during normal contact, yet his lack of genuine self-acceptance prevents him from fully exposing his deepest feelings, love, sensations, and thrills. He is more apt to quietly sigh than to scream. He is more likely to smile than to laugh. He is more inclined to say, "Yes, okay", instead of "Let's try this."

Surprisingly, the pleaser is moderately frigid sexually, although not as frigid as the avoider. The pleaser is warm as a friend, but when he gets into bed, his feelings go dead. His lack of inner trust, his void of self-love inhibits him from giving genuinely of himself. This is required for climactic sexual pleasure. Thus, the pleaser lacks the joy of complete sexual sensation to a great extent.

The Pleaser Has a Reservoir of People-Pleasing Talents

He Releases Tensions with Good Humor To gain approval, the pleaser devotes great efforts to develop his skills in "people pleasing." For example, he is astute at telling jokes and making clever comments. Whenever things are tense, he brings forth an effective tension-releasing observation. He has a tremendous ability to insert an unusual twist or humorous touch to get you to relax on almost any occasion.

He Is Sensitive The pleaser is aware of the nonverbal expressions people use to communicate, and thus is able to predict their responses well. This makes him highly sensitive to others' feelings and skillful at anticipating their reactions. Indeed, he is a virtual library of information about the interpersonal relationships and sensitive issues within an organization.

He Is Kind His people-pleasing behavior leads him to be very kind. He does numerous favors for you, and is available when you need him. He is polite and concerned, gives many gifts, and sends cards for every occasion. He is one of the few friends who remembers your birthdays and anniversaries, and who can get angry for long at a person who constantly bears gifts?

He Is the "Good Guy" Another skill the pleaser possesses is the ability to be a "good guy." Relatively nondefensive and nonaggressive when attacked, the pleaser acts hurt instead of angry. He seems to say, "Gee, why did you go and do that to me? I like you. Please like me. What can I do for you to make you feel better, to make you happy?" This nonevaluative posture of the pleaser encourages positive behavior from others in return. He is well liked because of this, but still only moderately respected.

When you are in the mood to relax, you enjoy the pleaser, because he does not expect any particular performance from you. When you are not in the mood for fun and games, however, the pleaser's behavior strikes you as inappropriate. This especially occurs at work when pressures to produce restrict the time for leisurely relations. Thus, many workers, especially more performer-oriented or commander-driven individuals, do not respect the pleaser for his productive efforts.

The Pleaser Performs Well in Social Tasks

The pleaser performs extremely well on jobs in which the key ingredient is pleasing others in social relationships. For example, a public relations position, airline ticket agent, or a salesman who maintains friendly contacts with customers would be highly appropriate jobs for the pleaser. These roles require someone who is positive and conciliatory. When asked to describe his job, the pleaser comments:

> I work with the greatest people you could ever meet. We are really close. Everyone gets along well. We seldom fight. We spend a lot of time away from work together. We usually play golf on Sundays. Our wives have coffee with each other all the time. It's great.

When given an assignment, the pleaser chooses friends rather than experts to work with him. In contrast, the achiever selects experts over friends, and the avoider chooses neither friends nor experts. He picks those who will cause him the least anxiety by following traditional ways of doing things.

The pleaser is a great listener but often does not take much action. One officer of a university commented:

> We will sit down to discuss a problem in his department, work it all through. He is agreeing all the time. He leaves my office and I say to myself, "Great, we got that one licked. He's going back to really straighten it out." Two weeks later he hasn't done a thing. He gets you all excited because he listens so well, agrees, and then you think he'll take all of the initiative required to implement the project. But nothing happens. If I go down and work with him on it step by step, we'll get it done. But I don't have the time to do it for him.!

The pleaser usually has few hobbies, skills or outside interests, and typically does an average job with those pursuits he does follow. If he takes up a new sport such as golf or tennis, he plays it for the social aspects of the game rather than the competitive dimensions. The pleaser is more concerned with making friends through recreation, while the performer wants to gain prestige. The achiever desires fulfillment by mastering the game itself, and is little interested in pleasing others. The avoider, on the other hand, wants to play the sport in such a way that he can hide most easily. He may play alone or with a shy, more silent and retiring group than the pleaser.

Another way of comparing the pleaser's performance to the others is to ask the question, "What would the pleaser do if he finished all of his work for the day by three in the afternoon?" He would probably walk around to find someone to shoot the breeze with. If possible, he would like to go fishing, golfing, to work around the house, or to be with his family. The performer would look immediately for another job to do. The avoider would sit in his office and worry.

Thus, the pleaser is an excellent producer on "social-skill jobs," a poor performer on high-risk, challenging jobs which demand self-reliance, initiative and self-responsibility. He is a moderate producer on assignments where he can be closely involved in a group, for then his needs to please can be fulfilled by his close times to his team, no matter what the task. Don Corleone in *The Godfather* displayed many of these skills in doing kind gestures and then collecting his "debts" when he was in need, albeit in a rather perverse way.

The pleaser takes low risks. If he has to set a goal, he usually chooses one that he is about 75 percent sure of attaining. It is difficult to measure the degree of risk in the pleaser's goals because he frequently accepts those of his peers, even though they may be much higher or lower than he prefers personally. Many times the pleaser's colleagues will be highly involved with achievement-related pursuits. Thus, to be accepted by the group, he must work toward their goals. He does so, however, by being a follower, not a leader.

The Pleaser Has Average Psychological Health

Outwardly, the pleaser appears well-adjusted and contented. Inwardly, he is nagged by self-doubt, feelings of inadequacy, and a basic mistrust of himself in most aspects of his life—from his theories of life to his skills in his career. That he is more self-confident than the avoider is demonstrated by his willingness to become involved with others and seek direction and acceptance from friends.

His acceptance need, however, is more a sick dependence, a need to be cared for, a lack of self-satisfaction which he seeks to fill through others rather than through a healthy enjoyment of mutually enriching relationships. His inward vacuum of loneliness is the source of his cravings for acceptance. One executive said:

My vice-president for personnel strikes me as being a genuine, classic pleaser. He excels at it, too. But, I'll be damned if I can tell whether or not he has self-confidence. On one hand, he seems to be very peaceful with himself and he's a pretty relaxed guy. Yet, on the other hand, he conforms to any group readily. And then I can tell a lot of times he's using me to reassure himself. I get the feeling sometimes that he's like a little kid in an adult's body. He almost seems vulnerable and tender, but then he goes sailing along, happy, joking with others.

Accordingly, his humor and pleasantness are vehicles to soften his lack of self-acceptance. The pleaser does not rely on his own judgment, for he feels it is inferior. Being alone with himself is a shattering experience. He copes with his inner hollowness by losing himself in crowds. Accordingly, I rank the pleaser as 50 out of 100 percent psychologically healthy. Compared with the achiever, he has reached half his human potential for fulfillment. Compared with the avoider he is almost three times as fulfilled.

The pleaser's positive dimensions are that he is gentle and pleasant to be around. He attempts to build others' egos, to approve of others' values and actions. Seldom, if ever, does he express a harsh word. For these reasons, the pleaser is easy to relax with, for you feel no matter what you do he will go along with you. In addition, he makes some effort to control his destiny. He does not completely withdraw as the avoider does. Correspondingly, he is much healthier than the avoider.

SUMMARY

Looking back at your rankings of ten friends in Chapter 1, which person has the highest needs to please? How well does the analysis presented in this chapter fit him? How extensive are your own needs to please?

Please try to summarize the eight major characteristics of a pleaser. Can you remember them, at least translate them into your own terms, without looking back over the chapter? After you have tried this, compare your answers with those presented in this chapter.

1. Overcaring
2. needs to be accepted
3. Other directed
4. Highly persuadable
5. Passive lover
6. People pleasing talents { Humor
   Sensative
7. good at social tasks   { nice
   Good guy
8. Average Psycological health

CHAPTER 6

The Performer

When the bellhop closed the door, Eric glanced at the plush view of the Pacific Ocean from his Hawaiian hotel, then told his wife he was going to check around. He immediately combed every corner of the resort and aimed for the registration desk to use his charm to persuade the clerk to give him the best room in the house. After switching rooms and downing lunch, Eric set about to surf, play tennis, and work on an overdue report before dinner.

At the age of thirty-one, Eric had climbed far in the investment business on the West Coast. He had worked hard all his life. During high school, for instance, he remained after football practice to run two extra miles. He excelled in his summer sales jobs in a large appliance business. Although his parents were middle-class, Eric worked his way into the upper social group in his high school and remained there during college and later in his community.

At Eric's parties, the guest list always included some important and influential community figures. "If you were invited you felt important," commented one of Eric's friends, "for you always knew you could rub elbows with some key names." His friend continued, "I always feel like I'm getting ahead when I'm with Eric, either at a party or work, but I never really have fun. People are always kind of strained or phony around him."

Eric had a need to perform. Who do you know personally that most resembles Eric? Write his initials here. _____ What is his style of living? _____ How does he relate to people? _____

How important is prestige to him? _____ *high*
How much does he strive for recognition and success? _____ *& highly*

How does he behave at a social gathering? _____ *Intelligent*

How do you like him? _____ *Not well*
How similar are you to Eric? _____ *Not - but like success*
_____ *& some prestige*

I believe the most pervasive psychological need within our society is to perform. Typically, the performer is the smoothest operator, the shrewdest politician, and the most polished social striver you know. Suave and clever, the performer manipulates his way to success. President Johnson's dramatic public performances—which ultimately created his ''credibility gap''—exemplify some of these traits. Similarly, President Nixon's derisive nickname "tricky Dick" grew from some of these same apparent characteristics. The flamboyant Huey Long, the governor of Louisiana in the 1930s, splashed his way across the state as a performer-leader.

The performer craves success because he needs approval from others to fill what he lacks in self-confidence. He strives with a life's commitment to perform outstanding feats and to reach prestigious positions.

You might compare the story you wrote about the picture in chapter 1 with the following one written by Eric. He observed:

> This group just finished designing a new investment package that will sell to old people with a lot of cash. They are saying, ''We will appeal to their need to protect against inflation by talking only about that issue. It's the same package as we sell to all groups of people, so we don't have any change in our overhead.'' The man standing is the boss. The one sitting in the center, Kirk, invented the concept and sold it to the group. His boss is saying to himself, ''Boy, I have a top man here. I'm going to give him special attention. He's about ready for a new promotion.'' Kirk feels thrilled because he knows he's made a hit.

The Performer's Training Environment Stresses Being Successful and Proper

The parents of the performer (and his other training agents) are very status conscious and perceive their child as an extension of themselves. Accordingly, they want him to make good impressions on others. The child is pushed to succeed at whatever he does, to grow up and "be somebody." When the child excels, his parents give him moderate praise but add, "And here is how you can improve next time." The child seldom is made to feel he is fully accepted and genuinely worthy. He is not accepted for what he is!

Since performer parents withhold authentic praise, their child feels incomplete. He feels he is not quite good enough to trust himself. Consequently, he tries to prove to himself and to others that he is great, so they will give him praise and build up his weak self-image.

The parents start early to ensure that their child attends the correct schools and associates with only the proper friends. The parents engineer their children's friendship patterns by discouraging unacceptable friendships with subtle innuendo or by making it inconvenient for their child to see these acquaintances.

In addition, they make decisions which pertain to their children by feigning participation. They design the most prestigious activities for their child, then subtly guide him to perform these tasks. When their teen-age daughter, for example, asks if she can go to the beach with her friends without a chaperone, her parents do not answer yes or no. If they do not want her to go, they manage to schedule a "family vacation" during the same time, get some other parent to kill it, or find some way to "talk her out of it." They do not give their honest reasons in an open conversation, for they do not want to risk appearing domineering or mean. By keeping their convictions hidden, they can more easily manipulate their image.

When their children misbehave, performer parents do not show displeasure. Instead, they give sly hints, joking suggestions, or half-hearted tips. Saying things tactfully becomes a rationalization for hiding honest feelings.

This artificial flavoring in the feedback that performer parents give their child causes their compliments to lose some of their value. One child reacted to her father's excessive praise with the insightful remark that, "Here's Daddy, telling me what a good girl I am all the time, and I didn't even do anything."

When conflicts occur between parents and their child, the performer parent smooths them over. Rather than facing problems directly as an achiever does or cutting them off as a commander does, he indirectly works on them.

A nine-year-old girl accidently found one of her father's *Playboy* magazines and asked in a rather disappointed tone, "Why do you read that, Daddy?" He looked stunned, and mumbled and said in a calm tone, "I really haven't read it. Someone just gave it to me as a joke, and I've been meaning to get rid of that trash and thought we had." Actually, he subscribed regularly, reading it from cover to cover. He could not, however, bring himself to admit to an action which might lessen his image. The daughter, sensing that her father was hedging, learned by example to distort the truth to maintain her appearance.

An illustration of the deliberate evasion of conflict by performer parents occurred when a family with two sons took a vacation. After several hours in the car, the sons got noisy and active. The father asked them repeatedly to settle down, but they did not. Finally, he lost his temper, turned around and slapped them. He suddenly became embarrassed by his actions, tried to make believe he had only been kidding, to joke with them and let them slap his hands. He did not apologize or explain why he had done it. Instead he tried to deny his real anger.

Finally, performer parents teach their children to be normal, tactful modifiers of the truth. A little girl at the swimming pool asked her mother, "Mommy, mommy can I have a Coke?" She replied, "No dear, I don't have any money." The little girl looked into her purse and said, "Yes, you do mommy, look here!"

Another little boy asked his performer father, "Dad, can I have a candy bar from that machine?" "No, son," he replied, "there aren't any more." Just then another child plugged in his money and out popped a candy bar. The child looked at his father in dismay. The child learns to transfer this style of behavior to other occasions and says to himself, "This is the way to get your wishes without causing problems. You just manipulate people." Accordingly, he generalizes his imposter behavior to most of his roles as an adult—to his marriage, children, work, recreation and friends.

A person's friends, job, spouse, and culture could provide similar training for this model of performer parents. If the parents did not provide this performer training, an individual could still receive it from many combinations of additional sources. We are using the parents as the primary example here.

The Performer Is an Explorer

The performer craves to explore his environment, to try our new ideas, to experiment, and to analyze why he succeeded or failed so he can do better next time. He is always on the move. At a party, he finds it difficult to sit still. He looks for something to do, for an important person to impress in a conversation, for something new to conquer. When he walks, he moves at a fast pace. He usually eats in a flurry, often unaware of what he is devouring. Even on vacation, after he is settled in his room, he searches every aspect of the resort—facilities, activities, and things he can do.

Because he plans each performance thoroughly, he anticipates his future and stresses the importance of time. Since he has above-average self-confidence, he is willing to plan ahead because he is optimistic about his chances for success. When he reaches his objectives, he begins to plan again. In contrast, avoiders, pleasers, and attackers frequently do not think ahead, for they are fearful they will not accomplish their goals.

The dynamism of the performer's behavior is expressed clearly in his aggressive actions. He walks with speed, tension, alertness, readiness to switch directions, to hear his name called, to jump into action. He bolts up stairs, frequently taking them two at a time. He juggles many different activities, is often interrupted by one of his numerous contacts or commitments. A large part of his day is usually spent in committee meetings, sales calls, or discussions.

His sleep is irregular, because it is often interrupted by quick thoughts of solutions to his consuming problems. Many nights, the performer finds himself up during the early hours writing down ideas. While shaving, driving to work, doing the dishes or cleaning the house, the performer frequently thinks of things he can do to make a hit. His mind darts from subject to subject, often leaving thoughts incomplete.

Similarly, the performer does several things simultaneously. While watching TV, he might read the newspaper, talk to his wife, and direct his children. These multiple actions allow him to use his time wisely, to get the biggest payoff for his investment of energy—as one government researcher phrases it, "to get the biggest bang for your bucks!"

In conversations, the performer selectively hears the things he can use to perform better. He goes to the heart of an issue, selects the main points and ignores the rest. Consequently, people often feel rejected, manipulated and "unheard" by the performer, unless he is trying to sell them.

The Performer Is Skillful at Manipulation

To reach great successes, the performer develops special talents in maneuvering others. These skills include pseudoparticipation, making special deals, cooperating with other performers, taking credit for successes, and parceling out compliments.

He Uses Pseudoparticipation One of his most salient maneuvering skills is to engage people in "pseudoparticipation." When making a decision, he calls a meeting and asks for his subordinates' ideas to make them feel like part of his team. After the meeting, he ignores most of their suggestions. By getting subordinates partially involved, he hopes to make them feel important and to remove their resistance to change. His insincerity, however, weakens his effectiveness.

He Is a Deal King The performer is extremely astute at the "if-then technique." *If* you do this for him, *then* he will do that for you. An officer of the largest bank in one southern town, for example, was approached from the United Fund who offered a crafty deal to the banker. *If* the banker would lead the fund drive, *then* the performer would run for the local city council and help pass legislation favorable to the bank. Often the performer works out these deals subtly. He hints about a deal until he finds approval for it so that he can back off if it is rejected.

He Engages in Joint-Image-Management The performer gets others to join him in a team effort to manage their images. He does this by first selecting from his friends and work associates those who are most likely to join his team—other performers. Then he lavishes great praise on his teammates in public.

When one of his teammates enters a group, therefore, someone is likely to say, "Oh, yes, you're Peter Brown. Jim has said so many nice things about you. He thinks you're great." Peter is pleased by these remarks and the next chance he gets, he returns the favor. He praises the originating performer, Jim, in public and the same process is set in motion. They both know they are working well together as a team, yet neither acknowledges it openly.

He Takes Credit for Successes If a project is received well, the performer artfully gains as much credit for its initiation as he can. If a plan fails, however, he treats it as if it were a stranger. Likewise, if there is a dirty job to do, he gets you to do it, while selecting positive tasks for himself."

He Parcels Out His Compliments The performer compliments only one person in a group for a particular talent, for he knows if he were to flatter several individuals in the same group, they would begin to say, "His words aren't worth much." Therefore, he rations his praise.

He Uses Anticipatory Socialization Because the performer wants to project an impressive image, he develops great talent in "anticipatory socialization." He develops skills in learning the norms of the status group above him and then acts as they do in order to be accepted more quickly by them.

This occurs frequently, for example, when the performer from the lower socioeconomic classes acquires sudden wealth. He buys a showy car, flashy clothes, and an ostentatious home. After arriving at this state, he soon anticipates his next stage of movement. He discovers that the upper-classes look down on gaudy displays of wealth. They prefer to manage their image through the inconspicuous demonstrations of "quality." By driving old cars, owning old but expensive homes, by not showing wealth, they can indicate they do not need it. The performer discovers this more quickly than others and soon shifts his living style to more genteel patterns of display.

He Uses Proper Timing When pay raise time comes around, the performer is the first to start a self-marketing program to maximize his increases. He steps up his attention to his boss, puts in extra hours, does the little extras to impress. As one observant manager in a steel manufacturing firm said,

> One of my men turns to the most unusual activity when raise time rolls around. I watched him for years and finally realized that it is almost like he's in heat. Usually he doesn't take work home with him at night. But a month or so before promotion period he takes his brief case out of the closet, dusts it off and hauls it around with him wherever he goes.

He Is an Inside-Dopester To manage his image, the performer assiduously collects current information regarding important topics—he becomes an "inside-dopester." If you want the latest inside information on who's doing what to whom, you turn to the performer. Points are won with his audience by his possession of valuable "gossip." When you attempt to do the same in a group of which he is a member, he is usually able to say, "Yes, and in addition. . . ." He can go beyond your insights and bring forth a storehouse of juicy facts and quotes. If he wants to know something, he does not ask you directly, as the achiever would. Instead, he seeks information deviously by questioning some of your friends, or your secretary, or observing you secretly.

He Is Counterclever And A One-Upsman The performer excels at rolling with the punches. If someone asks him a question which he is embarrassed about, he comes up with an appropriate face-saving response instantly in a calm, quick, though somewhat counterfeit manner. One Ivy League college coach remarked about his star performer quarterback, "He can change his direction without losing a step!"

He is also a master at counterpunching. If someone tells an enthralling story, for instance, he always joins in with a clever, witty observation or an ironical twist to the story.

He Is Hard to Pin Down—A Fence Sitter The performer is hard to pin down about his personal beliefs, because overtly he goes along with the most popular ideas, yet keeps his true beliefs private so he will not offend anyone and thus block his climb upward. He says almost anything as long as it will help him come out on top. One naval officer said this about a performer in his unit:

He'll tell a man that he's great, he likes what he's done and that he wants to promote him. But then when he is with his supervisor he changes his story completely if his supervisor disagrees. You get the feeling you can't trust him. He is slippery. But, then he often seems to have a sound argument to support everything he does. So you say to yourself, "Maybe he was right to change his mind."

The Performer Masters Sensation Transference The performer understands well the concept of sensation transference—the process of transferring first impressions about an object into feelings about its contents. When you see a package, you get a sensation. If you like it, you develop a favorable sensation. You then transfer this sensation into the contents of the package. This is why, for example, so many products that we put close to our mouths—toothpastes, soap, Kleenex—are packaged in soft, clean pastel colors and gentle textures. We do not like to wash our face with a product whose package gives us a greasy, rough sensation. Likewise, when we see a beautiful girl, we get a sensation and transfer our feelings into our beliefs about her personality. Whatever she says sounds brilliant.

The performer is a master at creating positive sensations which he wants you to transfer to his personality. He uses his keen sense of judgment at every turn to ensure that he is there at the right time, in the right place, with the right remark, and cultivating the right image. The following are some of the sensation transference techniques he uses.

He Controls Information Because the performer wants to be unobtrusive in his cunning acts, he controls the information available to those with whom he relates by letting out only that which will enhance his position and by smothering information which might be harmful. He controls access to his inner regions so you see only the performance, the artificial man, not the real person.

Professor Anthony Athos, for instance, has drawn the following example of the performer-professor during the first day of a class.

The professor is worried about how he will appear on this first encounter, so he enters the classroom with several books under his arms, some official papers, and an air of "I know plenty. You lucky devils; here I am!" The materials he carries are both a shield to protect him and to impress the students.[1]

As the class settles, the professor pretends to straighten his papers on the table, but is secretly looking around the room to discover the tough guys and the friendly students. He begins class by letting out his tensions, telling the students how hard he is going to be, and describing the tests, grades and other rewards and punishments he controls. Then he moves into the course content by making a few statements and asking for reactions from the class, for by all means, he wants to have open discussions. Silence is broken only by one of the smiling faces who wants to please by offering a comment to break the ice. Meanwhile, the three fraternity brothers sitting in the back are asking, "How can I relate to this guy? What is going to happen to me in here?" One of these men, a performer, starts to get interested and almost raises his hand, but suddenly catches the glances of his two brothers. He says to himself, "I'd better gauge this a little more carefully before I risk getting involved and getting kidded back at the house." The professor continues by trying to put on a good performance for his audience.

He Is Purposefully Courteous To ensure that others do not intrude on his behind-the-scenes activities, the performer carefully ignores others' staged activities—he tactfully does not see an indiscretion; he does not hear a slip of the tongue; he readily accepts a lame excuse; he coughs before he enters a room to warn others who may be talking about him that he will soon be near. Because he is sensitive to hints, he leaves the shadow of a jest in his voice. He pretends not to hear when the receptionist discusses with her boss over the phone whether to let him in or not. As a result, his privacy is respected in repayment for his courtesy.

An interesting example of this process is a high class prostitute's use of deception in her professional relationships. One such performer explained how she pleased her clients:

1. Lecture by D. Anthony Athos, Harvard Business School, given to School of Business, University of North Carolina, Fall, 1968.

I do what I know they want, make believe I'm ga-ga over them. Sometimes they act like little boys playing games. Mr. Blakessee always does. He plays the cave man. He comes to my apartment and sweeps me in his arms and holds me till he thinks he's taken my breath away. It's a howl. After he's finished making love to me, I have to tell him, "Darling, you made me so happy I could just cry." You wouldn't believe a grown-up man would want to play such games, but he does. And it's not only him, but most of the rich ones. (Erving Goffman, *The Presentation of Self in Everyday Life*, 1959)

Hers is a professionalized performer role, much like many of the careers of acting, singing, and entertaining. The truly great actor reaches the pinnacle of acting when the audience cannot tell he is acting. When he appears real, he is good.

He Dresses Properly By being perfectly groomed, dressed fashionably, and by observing the correct custom for any occasion, the performer packages himself well. This, of course, is relative to a given situation. The young performer may wear dirty, droopy, wild clothes, but he is in perfect fashion for his peer group. Similarly, a debutante performer, who wears the latest in expensive dress, jewelry, and shoes, maximizes her image for her peers.

He Selects Proper Friends The performer also enhances his image by selecting the proper friends to be seen with at the best times. Again, this is relative to his peers' norms. The performer who is a businessman frequently engineers public appearances with community leaders. The young rebel performer appears in the best hangouts with the informal rebel leaders, singers, and youth heroes. His friendships are often artificial.

He Acquires Proper Knowledge The performer embellishes his image by acquiring the "proper" knowledge. He hates to be left out of a conversation because of ignorance. Accordingly, he reads the latest book, sees the current "in" movie, knows the most popular music, and draws upon these sources of information to make himself appear knowledgeable.

He Uses Proper Habits The performer drinks the proper drinks, eats the "in" foods, and partakes in the "right" forms of stimulants. He arrives at the fashionable time for his group, not the time that he would naturally be able to arrive, but the one that he senses is most acceptable. One college girl said:

> When I was a sophomore in high school, the time for our big school dance had arrived. Several of my performer friends told me they couldn't do anything all day Saturday because they had to get ready for the dance. So I thought I had better start getting ready early too so I would look great. I started at 4:00 in the afternoon and was ready by 4:30. I couldn't figure out what to do next so I got undressed and went up town to mess around until 7:30. The performer girls spent hours in grooming themselves for their appearance, however.

He Disguises His Efforts In each of these instances, the performer artfully disguises his concern for propriety so that he does not appear to be straining to look good. Above all, he seeks to convey the impression that his talents flow naturally from the "real me." He implies that he just casually read the latest book, just happened to buy the latest swimming suit. To appear too eager would be undignified. Consequently, people who do not know him well perceive his attributes as genuine indicators of the real inner person. Those who work with him intimately see the differences between the outward glitter and the inward vacuum. Visibility destroys his mirage.

He Uses Protective Devices When the performer's props are discovered, he is embarrassed. He attempts, therefore, to protect his inner self by shifting from one group to another. If he never gets close to others, he is better able to keep up his front. To pretend to be something you are not is an exhausting activity, for it is nearly impossible to be on guard at all times around close associates.

A good illustration of this protective device is the performer's behavior at a cocktail party. He approaches a small group in conversation, enters into the discussion, makes a few winning observations, drops a few names, and mentions the latest movie. Then, without warning, he disappears. He is off again, performing the same ritual with another group. He leaves while he is ahead. If you happen to be left alone with him, he politely carries the conversation for a respectful few moments, then shrewdly departs to "get another drink."

He Uses Two Aspects of Communication

There are two aspects of what a person communicates: (1) what he says, the verbal part, and (2) what he does, the nonverbal part. Verbal communication is more controllable than nonverbal. Thus, most of us unconsciously compare the consistency of what someone says with what he does. When someone says, "I'm so glad to see you," and then turns around and walks off, we become suspicious of what he said. Similarly, a housewife, who serves a meal to her guest, is often greeted by many compliments. If one of the guests says, "This is really great chicken," she still silently observes how quickly he eats, how much he leaves, whether his face expresses pleasure, or if he is strained while eating. By checking his verbal behavior against his nonverbal actions, she tries to determine his sincerity.

Because he is able to control his nonverbal communications, the performer is truly effective in managing his image. When expecting you for dinner, for example, the performer might keep his eyes glued to the window to observe your behavior as you approach his door. If you walk up the steps with a frown on your face and then put on a masked smile as the door opens, he senses your feelings and artfully says something to cheer you up, and hints that he observed the change in your nonverbal communications, thus he places you in the position of "owing" him something to compensate for your error. Since he is an expert himself, he sees through your attempts at image management and uses his expertise to enhance his own position. For these reasons, it is difficult to con a con man.

The Performer's Sexual Style

The thrill of conquest is more stimulating to the performer than is the sharing of a close personal love. While pursuing his partner, he is energized by the challenge, the contest, and the excitement. When his partner submits, this gives him proof that he is a good lover. Thus, for the performer, the means is generally more important than the end.

He only takes as much time in foreplay as is needed to sufficiently stimulate his spouse to succumb to his desires. He only shows as much affection, tenderness, and caring as is required at the moment to prove himself.

His style of making love is fleeting, distant; it is without intimacy. His warmth is superficial, his giving of himself is phony. Authentic sharing with his partner is difficult for him. He makes up for his aversion to honest intimacy by excelling in showmanship.

One car salesman, who was a performer, bragged how he had gone to a prospect's home to try to sell them a car. Finding that the husband was not home, he sensed that he could make a sexual conquest. He had a significant obstacle, however, because the lady's young children were actively playing around the house. So he engineered his female verification agent against the wall in the kitchen and had intercourse standing up.

In a training group seminar which this performer attended, as he relayed his gross conquest to the other male participants, I could not help but feel that he had been on a big game hunt, and would have hung his female target on the wall to demonstrate his skill if his wife would not have objected.

The Performer Bends the Truth

Not being a hard-core liar, but rather a gentle exaggerator, the performer stretches the truth. As one performer's wife said in defense of her husband, "He just doesn't say anything when he disagrees, so he really doesn't lie."

The performer has a way of exposing you to certain bits of information and drawing analogies so you will believe what he wants you to. Nevertheless, he maintains an escape hatch. He makes his point with just enough smile in his voice that if you react strongly, he can say he was just kidding or that you misunderstood him.

He Does Not Commit Himself By intentionally creating the impression he desires without getting himself into an indefensible position, the performer leaves himself uncommitted. If a wife performer, for example, wants her husband to read a book, she does not tell him to do so as the commander does or suggest it directly as an achiever would. Instead she leaves the book around the house in conspicuous places, drops casual hints about it, and brings it up in a passing conversation.

He Uses False Flattery   The performer secretly lies by flattering his boss and others when he does not mean it. When his boss tells a joke, he is ready with a hearty laugh, a knowing smile. He adopts the same work habits and customs of his boss. The restaurants and entertainment affairs that his boss attends are certain to magnetically draw the performer. When the boss is ready to break off a meeting or to leave a luncheon, the performer anticipates his moves and is on his feet the split second after his boss arises, even if he really feels like staying.

He Uses False Modesty   False modesty used at the right times with keen emphasis is also one of the performer's methods of easing around the truth. If it is obvious to all that he performed well, then he has nothing to lose and everything to gain to shedding praise with the hidden shield of, "It was the team," or "It really wasn't much."

He Lies to Himself   The final significant dimension of a performer's truth distortion is that he lies to himself. Since he does not accept the perceptions of his subordinates, he cannot see himself as a foxy, tricky person who strives for success to gain approval. He does not listen to the messages his friends or subordinates are trying to give him. He tends to see himself as an achiever—tactful, honest, straightforward.

Also, the performer does not accept the definition given here of a performer. He says, "Well, really, when you get right down to it the performer just adapts to each new situation appropriately. He is just a creative manager, a catalyst. And what is this lying bit? Just because you hold back your opinions does not mean you are a liar." When asked by his wife, "What does it mean then?" One performer commented, "Oh, it just means that you, ah . . . ah are trying not to hurt people." She responded to her husband:

That may be why you think you lie, but isn't it still a lie to hide your true feelings, to not disagree openly when you really do, to hold back praise when you want to give it, not to let out anger when it is boiling inside you? I'm not saying this is good or bad. I'm just trying to define what is and is not a lie. What I hear you saying, dear, is that you think it is okay to lie in certain situations.

He reacted by saying, "Yeah, but it is not lying when you are really, ah, just not saying anything."

The Performer Does Well in Prestigious Jobs

The performer is most successful in jobs involving only moderately close contacts with others. He does best when a first impression is important, when a flashy, polished image gets the job done, and when the positions are challenging and prestigious. Banking, promotion, sales, public relations, politics, general management, and especially advertising, fit nicely with the performer's personality needs. When he can impress without giving his audience time to see beneath his facade, then he can be effective and successful.

The performer does not wait for things to happen to him. He maneuvers astutely to keep himself on top of a situation. He foresees the probable consequences of his actions and then initiates his winning combination of shrewd actions. William Whyte's example of the performer-waitress points to this characteristic nicely:

> The skilled waitress tackles the customer with confidence and without hesitation. For example, she may find that a new customer has seated himself before she could clear off the dirty dishes and change the cloth. He is now leaning on the table studying the menu. She greets him and says, ''May I change the cover please?'' and without waiting for an answer takes his menu away from him so that he moves back from the table, and she goes about her work. The relationship is handled politely but firmly, and there is never any question as to who is in charge. (Whyte, p. 19)

This example suggests how the performer does what he wants and yet manages not to make you feel too controlled. In fact, he can almost make you think it was your suggestion in the first place, that he is merely carrying out your wishes.

One woman indicated that a performer-mother carried out this act to perfection. She convinced the mothers that they should give their minister's daughter a shower for her forthcoming marriage. The date of the shower was set one day before the performer's own daughter's sixteenth birthday party. Both the shower and the birthday party were to be held at the performer's house. She structured each mother's contribution so that each brought a large amount of flowers, decoration, and food. In fact, it was enough for two parties. And indeed the performer mother used the "leftovers" for her daughter's party the following day.

Several of the mothers later said, "You know, I wondered why she was so adamant about my bringing certain kinds of foods. I think we were taken." These afterthoughts point up one of the dilemmas of the performer's efforts. Usually the performer engineers the results he wants; but after several occurrences, those who were deceived realize it and become leery. One man said of his boss, a performer,

> You really have to watch him. He'll act like he is doing you the nicest favor in the world and suddenly you are standing there, your wallet is gone, your pockets are picked and you're naked. The crazy part of it is that you have a smile on your face, for you know you have been robbed by an expert. You are so amused at seeing a master imposter strip you, that you forget you're the victim because you admire his craft.

This subordinate continued to comment,

> Most of us who know him well can see through his facade. But we're afraid to say this to outsiders because if he finds out, he'll get us. We won't know where the arrows will be coming from, but we'll get shot for sure. Most of those who don't know him well respect him. And you have to give him credit. He gets more done than most people. I guess the only thing that bothers me is the way he goes about doing it.

The performer, therefore, reaches high positions, produces significant results, yet creates mistrust. The performer schemes to get ahead, while the achiever, for example, openly works on problems because they are important to him. The commander dominates; the pleaser cooperates. The performer defines success in terms of how much prestige, influence, and recognition he receives. The achiever defines success on the basis of how meaningful and helpful the results are to others. The achiever feels good when he does what he believes regardless of the results. The commander measures success in terms of order, control, and domination; the pleaser in terms of friendships.

The performer takes risks for which he has an above average chance of succeeding, regardless of whether he enjoys the tasks or thinks they are meaningful. When the tasks are important, the achiever takes risks which have about a 50 percent chance of succeeding, whereas the commander and pleaser seek tasks on which they have a 75 percent chance of success.

The performer, typically, is overextended in work, community, and social commitments. He runs from one obligation to another without stopping to breathe deeply. Consequently, he often finds himself unable to do all of his jobs well, behind on his deadlines, under pressure to hurry, and living life as an emergency.

This hyperactivity explains why he seldom sits still, for if he does so he misses opportunities to perform, to prove his worth, and thus gain recognition to satisfy his lack of self-confidence. Accordingly, his overextension contributes to his fleeting, distant relationships with his wife, children, friends, and work associates.

To spend time in purposeless tasks—having fun or enjoying himself in some expressive behavior—is the height of wastefulness for the performer. If a human encounter does not pay off in a direct benefit by teaching him how to perform better or making some successful output, he ignores it.

It is important to note that the performer seeks to excel at whatever goals his peer group defines as prestigious. In some cases, he might try to appear as a "super-balanced family man" by spending much time at home, appearing in the "right" places with his children, going to church regularly, or doing his "family service and business chores" respectfully. In other cases, a teen-aged performer, for example, might strive to dress, talk, and behave to perfection according to his youth group's norms. This might vary from being an intellectual to an anti-intellectual. Whatever the content of the performer's life style, his process of living is artificial and compulsive.

Similarly in whatever he does the performer calculates the odds of his success so that he has a high chance of winning on a prestigious pursuit. He needs to win to look good. Consequently, he is not a gambler.

One performer, in discussing this, mentioned that when he had just graduated from college, he took a tour West, stopping in Las Vegas. During the evening he gambled on craps until 3:00 A.M. He won $84 and retired to his room while he was ahead. But, as he put it, "My fingers got to itching so bad to go back, they actually started to twitch. So I packed and left town by 3:30 A.M. and drove all the way to Los Angeles. It's like a disease there. There's no way you can win, but the excitement, lights, noise and drinks get to you." Nonperformers, especially avoiders, might have succumbed to the contagion and returned to the craps table.

The Performer Has Average Psychological Health

The performer's lack of genuine psychological health is indicated by his conspicuous, obsessive attempts to prove himself to others. Lacking inner acceptance, he needs to demonstrate his talents publicly so others will pat him on the back, give him deference, act jealous about his accomplishments, and thereby give the performer what he lacks—self-esteem. He needs bundles of praise, for he cannot find the feelings of satisfaction from within himself. Yet he is more self-contained than the four previously discussed personality types.

The performer's cravings for recognition and respect drive him to make great sacrifices in his marriage, health, and children. During many sleepless nights, his self-doubts and anxieties twist his stomach. He does not feel contented. Rather, tension is his constant companion; restlessness is his prevailing mood. Yet his unhappiness with himself does not allow him to cease performing. He does, however, control his life and feels better about himself than most other personality types. I rank performers, therefore, as 65 out of 100 percent psychologically healthy. This number, of course, merely indicates my judgment of the relative rank of performers compared to the other five types. It suggests a matter of degree.

The performer's positive attributes are that he is more self-contained and self-reliant than the commander, attacker, avoider, and pleaser. He desires to improve greatly, and is somewhat creative. He thinks about his own self-actualization, and I strongly believe that unconsciously he is aware of his special problems and wishes that he were different. These thoughts of self-actualization, however, frighten the performer, for to let himself go too far in considering the possibilities of genuine psychological health would derail him from his main mission—to perform and to receive recognition. Consequently, he never quite faces the frightening thought that his excessive striving is to prove himself over and over again.

SUMMARY

Look back at your list of ten friends you analyzed in chapter 1 and determine how many of them have a dominant need to perform. How accurately do the descriptions provided in this chapter fit the performers you can name? How do you like them?

To help in your mastery of understanding performers, see how well you can recall and summarize the seven major characteristics.

1. How was the performer raised? _Stress being proper & successful_

2. How does the performer exploit his environment? _Manipulation_

3. How does he manipulate others? _Deal Maker_

4. How does he master sensation transference? _Creates positive Sensations_

5. How does he bend the truth? _Yes_

6. In what kind of jobs does the performer do well? _Prestigious_

7. How psychologically healthy is the performer? _65%_

CHAPTER 7

The Achiever

When people met Bill they wanted to be his friend. People clustered around him, visited him, for they desired to be close to him. Why? The answer is not what you would expect. He was not wildly brilliant, brash, rich, handsome, or strange in any of the more glamorous ways. He was average in most of these characteristics.

The qualities which made Bill a magnetic force were his acceptance of others, his curiosity, laughter, warmth, serene movements, calm smile, and honesty. He thought deeply about issues and held strong but not dogmatic convictions.

Bill started his own real estate company after working his way through college by selling cars and later real estate. After ten years of running his own firm and actively helping in his community, Bill had acquired wealth and respect, but not at the expense of enjoying his life thoroughly. Bill's goals were to develop quality residential areas (ones with beauty, recreational, and spatial designs), to make a reasonable profit, and to have fun. Making money, controlling others, being popular, hiding or gaining prestige were not his goals.

When asked what were the keys to his success, Bill responded, "It is very simple. Tell people the truth and exactly what you are going to do. Then do what you said you would do." Bill's high quality reputation in his community attested to the fact he carried out these beliefs. Bill is a person I classify as an achiever.

Who do you know that most resembles Bill? He need not be in

business, but can be in any walk of life. Write in his initials here.
_____ What style of life does he live? _____
How do people feel about him? _____

How much self-confidence does he have? _____

How does he relate to others? _____

How does he approach his work, leisure and family? _____

People who have a high need to achieve are self-confident. Consequently, they try to reach their potential and to master meaningful tasks rather than to gain applause, prestige, or money, although frequently, they receive these rewards because of their natural talents.

One achiever wrote the following story about the picture in chapter 1:

> These people are thinking about the pleasure they feel after just developing one of the finest new biology programs in the United States. They feel that future generations will benefit greatly from making biology more relevant and exciting to students, for ultimately it will help to solve ecological problems that must be overcome for the world to be a good place to live. They worked hard but enjoyed what they were doing.

Be he the carpenter who is thrilled when he builds an excellent cabinet, the mother who sees her child blossom, the teacher who awakens bored students, or the company president who loves the press of competition, I have found that the achiever in any field is most content when he is working to master his challenges, to benefit others, and to achieve his potential. Historical examples of the achiever for you to consider, in my judgment, are Abraham Lincoln, Benjamin Franklin, and to a large degree, Franklin Roosevelt.

The Achiever's Environment Warmly Encourages Independence

Achiever parents typically encourage active participation from their children based on their physical and psychological abilities. They engage in two-way communication with them about those things that are relevant to their lives.

When a child asks if he can ride his bike on a busy street, his parents do not arbitrarily say yes or no. Rather, they ask the child, "Is this what you would like to do? Do you think it is safe? Do you know what it means to ride on busy street?" If, after the conversation, the parents feel it is not safe, they will say so and explain why. If they feel it is okay, they offer their suggestions clearly and honestly, and allow the child to ride. In either case, however, the decision is discussed.

At an early age, then, the child begins to feel that he is responsible for his behavior, develops self-confidence in guiding his actions, and feels warmth radiating from his parents.

His parents encourage, in a natural manner, self-reliance and independence. He is allowed to spend the night at a friend's house, to go to the movies, attend camps, and explore his environment at an earlier age than nonachievers. Remember the achiever-parent, cited in chapter 2, who told his daughter to find her own way to Long Island, using her own judgment. The commander parent gave detailed directions. Therein lies the difference.

One study showed, for example, that achiever mothers expected their eight-year-old sons (1) to master their way around the city; (2) to make their own friends; (3) to be active and energetic; (4) to try things for themselves; (5) and to do well in competition. Non-achiever parents started this only at later ages. (Winterbottom)

The achiever child, then, is accepted, made to feel he is "okay" (Harris, *I'm Okay, You're Okay*). He is not pushed prematurely, but encouraged to fly when he is ready. The performer, in contrast, is pushed hard before he is able to succeed competently. The achiever receives much accurate feedback about his performance and warmth and support in his personal relationships with his parents. Thus, he is willing to take risks, to venture out of his home and to fail. When he fails, he knows he will still be accepted warmly by his parents and helped to try again. If he succeeds, he is rewarded by praise. Soon he learns that he largely controls his own life. Since he feels good about himself, he asks, "Why be defensive, evasive, and shy?" He knows his weaknesses and strengths, and sets about to make the most of them. His parents set examples of doing the same in their own lives and encourage their child to follow their lead.

Achievers Have High Self-confidence

It is difficult for most of us to understand, but a true achiever's tank of self-confidence is full. The achievers I have studied are at peace with themselves. They lack overpowering guilt, crippling shame, or tense anxiety. They are not embarrassed about what they think, how much they know, who their friends are, what clothes they wear, what clubs they belong to, what their physical features are, or who their parents are. They accept their weaknesses without self-doubt and react to failures without self-punishment. They say to themselves, "Why regret my natural characteristics? I do not get mad because it rains. It is natural to have weaknesses. I can't help the way I am, even though I try to improve myself."

Because their parents have shown love and esteem for them, even in bad moments, achievers feel little guilt, shame, or anxiety at their everyday failings, for they know they are part of their natural make-up. For the same reason, they suffer no embarrassment over their physical features or their family origins. They can always say pretty much what they think with neither embarrassment nor compromise, even if they may be rather ignorant on a subject, for they are not compelled to impress, but simply to communicate.

In training groups, I typically ask the participants to write down their own good and bad points. Then, I ask them how much they "really" want to improve their weaknesses. Usually the achiever, because of his relative peace with himself, says, "Well, you know I wish I didn't have these bad points. I have been working on them and I'll continue to do so. . . . I just kind of accept them and try to do better." On the contrary, the nonachiever is very discouraged and worries a lot about his weaknesses.

Indications of achievers' high self-confidence are that they expect to do better on new projects than nonachievers. When asked how they expect to do on a final exam, college students who are achievers think they will do better than do nonachievers, even when they have both done the same in the past. Similarly, when achiever students are asked how many other students in their class they think they can beat at darts, shuffleboard, or other games, they estimate they will win more often than do nonachievers. (Atkinson, p. 164).

In a competitive situation, achievers perform well, while avoiders do poorly, because achievers are not overcome by anxiety. When they are getting ready to take an I.Q. test, for example, they are more relaxed and confident than nonachievers for they will not be crushed by negative outcomes (Heinz Heckhausen, *The Anatomy of Achievement Motivation*, 1967, p. 128).

Part of the reason for their self-confidence is that achievers acquired their personalities more from experiencing and thinking through their ideas for themselves rather than by being told what to think. Consequently, their values became connected in reasonable ways, and they developed an integrated personality. Their beliefs, therefore, are not disjointed and unconnected as are the commander's, for example. Commanders have been told what to think. Achievers learned to think for themselves.

They Are Self-Directed   Because achievers acquire their values by analyzing their experiences, they are not easily persuaded; they are self-reliant. They listen but also evaluate carefully. Commanders and attackers are also resistant to outside pressure, but they are closed-minded. They do not listen.

Entrepreneurs are famous for their confidence in the face of challenges. Alfred P. Sloan's analysis of General Motors' decision to continue Chevrolet production after the war illustrates this point well:

> The most illuminating recommendation was that the whole Chevrolet operation should be liquidated. There was no chance to make it a profitable business. We could not hope to compete. I was much upset because I feared the prestige of the office might overcome our arguments to the contrary, so I went to Mr. Pierre DuPont. . . . We urged . . . that it was an insult to say that we could not compete with anyone. It was a case of ability and hard work. He listened most patiently and finally said, ''Forget the report. We will go ahead and see what we can do!'' Mr. DuPont was always that way; he had the courage of his convictions. Facts were the only things that counted. (Sloan, p. 149)

DuPont and Sloan were not immobilized by the ambiguities and the risks involved. Rather, they relied on hard work and ability to produce the successful results they envisioned and eventually realized in the Chevrolet business.

They Are Nondefensive Since they accept themselves and acknowledge their weaknesses, I have found achievers to be relatively nondefensive. When criticized, they do not react violently as attackers do, withdraw as avoiders do, appease as pleasers do, control as commanders do, or maneuver as performers do. Achievers are open to differences of opinion and more able to accept criticism than most. Since they know their inner lives well and feel positive about their own character, they say to themselves, ''I have little to hide so why try to defend against my weaknesses?''

Since achievers desire to fulfill their potentials, they listen to others to find ways of growing. They are able to separate their personal biases from the content of the messages being delivered to them. They objectively evaluate the meaning of the personal feedback they receive and seek within themselves the reasons for their behavior.

The achiever feels he need not keep his doors locked when he knows what is beyond the gates. He has unlocked most of them himself many times before and has a large supply of positive feelings about himself to balance off the negative findings he might discover.

They Have An Acute Awareness of Their Inner Feelings Since they accept themselves and are relatively nondefensive, achievers have an intensive awareness of their inner feelings—their desires, motivations and subjective emotions (like feelings of hate and love). They are highly attuned to significant shifts in their reactions to a person or situation. They do not distort their feelings, try to hide them, project them onto others, or repress them. When they catch glimpses of their feelings, they say to themselves, ''Heh, something is going on inside of me. Now what is it I am feeling? Why am I thinking this way?'' Even quite negative ideas and fantasies are allowed to float up into their consciousness. They do not frighten achievers as much as unacceptable feelings disturb most of us. In this way, achievers learn to know themselves well.

Achievers Are Spontaneous and Natural

Achievers respond naturally and genuinely to their situations. Their behavior is uncluttered by worries of self-protection or image enhancement; therefore, they are in a kind of one-to-one relationship with their world, in harmony with their surroundings.

There is a childlike genuineness in the achievers' lack of calculation of how they should behave or what they should say next. Since they are unconcerned with others' opinions of them, they are able to express their real thoughts in what they say, feel, and do. They are expressive, for they need not plan how to act, but rather can let themselves respond spontaneously. They feel no need to guard each word or stylize each action; rather, they can open themselves for others to see. They can allow their deepest thoughts to be transparent, to flow out of themselves in words and deeds.

Accordingly, achievers' thoughts are easier to perceive since "what you see is what you get." They care little for artificial social customs of dress, hair styles, decor, proper manners, and customs of their peers. They feel that artificial traditions or fashions are relatively meaningless and unimportant, so they try to make them routine habits which require little premeditation (Maslow, p. 160). Achievers prefer the company of people who allow them freedom from conventions and to behave spontaneously.

Unlike performers, achievers do not need to conform to social conventions such as regular church attendance, up-to-date clothing styles, or familiarity with best sellers to determine their personal worth. Success as a fashionplate does not make a good person in the achiever's eyes. I have found that external criteria are relegated to a low position in their value hierarchies.

Their slight unconventionality is not done to defy authority as is the case for attackers, or to conform to a peer group of authority-rebels as might be the case for pleasers. Instead, it is a genuine lack of concern for others' evaluations of them by external standards. This self-authenticity may cause them to deviate from social custom, but not from their own values. They dislike making an effort to appear good; thus, they follow their natural impulses. If they can follow conventions without excessive effort, they do so. But if the customs interfere with their beliefs, they disregard them.

Achievers Are Self-reliant

Achievers rely on their own inner resources to guide their lives. They prefer to determine their fate rather than to be steered by others. Consequently, they dislike games of chance, gambling, or assignments which the boss dominates, or those in which the technology prevents them from exercising personal judgment. If a job does not allow individual initiative, even though it gives them a good chance for success, they do not enjoy it. Consequently, they devote little effort toward it unless it greatly benefits others.

One interesting research project, for example, showed how achievers avoid risk when the situation—like gambling—is beyond their own control. It found that in poker and craps achievers bet on those alternatives for which they had the surest chance of winning. Since they knew they could not rely on their own skills, they were unwilling to take risks (McClelland, p. 214).

Because they like challenge, achievers' self-initiative often turns dull jobs into exciting ones and launches achievers into bigger things. Upon graduation from college, Olin Larson took a job as an administrative assistant in a large firm. He was assigned to manage a file—a rather humble beginning for a man who aspired to be a top executive. But Larson searched for ways to insert his personality into his work. He developed a new index that was more useful for management. He interviewed top executives for new information to store, designed methods for implementing changes, and gained the cooperation of other departments. Soon he gained the eye of top management and was groomed for advancement (Zaleznik, p. 44).

He is Self-contained Achievers' self-reliance allows them to establish healthy dependent and independent relationships. They cooperate when the need arises, but also enjoy working by themselves. Being alone does not scare them; in fact, they enjoy privacy.

An interesting display of an achiever's self-containment occurred when a college president, who was an achiever, was browsing through a bookstore with his wife, who was a pleaser. They stopped in front of the ski books and simultaneously picked up a different book, turned to each other and exclaimed, ''Boy, does this look great!'' The cover of the book the wife selected displayed a husband, wife, and two children playfully skiing on a gentle slope. The cover of the book which attracted the husband showed a lone skier shunting through the air over a large peak. The president and his wife looked at each other and laughed. Here was a vivid illustration of their preferences for different types of pleasure—achieving versus pleasing.

Another illustration of achievers' self-containment was a husky, successful, forty-year-old executive who made a list of the top ten tennis players in his club so he could use them as a measure of his own improvement. He did not necessarily want to beat them but to gauge his progress by how well he played against them. His wife, who had a high need to please, looked over his shoulder at the list and asked, "Is that a list of friends you want to play with this year?" She perceived friendship; he saw challenge and the chance to achieve his potential.

The psychological autonomy of achievers sometimes makes them appear aloof, above the immediate crisis. They remain calm when most become anxious; they like solitude when others become lonely. Since achievers are more objective and problem-centered, they do not feel rejected if not included in every gathering or committee. Often they prefer to be by themselves, gradually losing patience with people who are striving to satisfy their needs to control, attack, avoid, please, or perform. This self-containment is reflected in their ability to sleep soundly, to laugh naturally during crises, and to not worry constantly when things are not going correctly.

Achievers Are Goal-oriented

Achievers set high expectations for themselves and want to make significant contributions to society. They are not possessed as performers are, however, with thoughts of, "How prestigious is this task?" "How big a return on investment will I gain for my time and efforts?" Or, "How good will it make me look?" I have found that achievers are motivated by intrinsic personal goals, by their genuine beliefs in what they are doing. The prestige of their work is of little concern as long as it provides fulfillment for them and contributes to others. In this way, they are quite altruistic.

Similarly, they are not possessed by their work to the degree performers are. Achievers work hard but in a more relaxed manner. They seem to be able to put their work in realistic perspective to their entire life. They do not feel crushing tensions when they fail, or lose their humility when they succeed. They are able to maintain a sense of humor in a crisis.

Achievers are able to obtain just enough stimulation to stay excited without overdoing it. Unlike performers, they do not consider job success the ultimate reflection of their worth. Thus, achievers feel more at ease in their work. They do only what they believe in. They view their efforts more as pleasure than as work.

Sometimes their immediate success may not be as apparent as performers, but their contribution and ultimate visibility is usually greater in the long run. They do not spend their time advertising their accomplishments.

Achievers Are Problem-centered Instead of Self-centered

Since achievers are not striving to fulfill the self-esteem vacuum most of us have, they are able to look beyond themselves, beyond their self-image and occasionally-bruised ego. Consequently, they are relatively free from self-centered concerns. They are not possessed by worries about needs to command, attack, avoid, please, or perform.

This freedom from self opens the world to them. They are more able to ask, "How meaningful are the things I am doing?" "Am I working on these tasks because I genuinely enjoy them or because I want to get ahead?" "How significant are the results of my efforts?" They can usually avoid consideration of questions such as "How safe, standardized, and traditional are my pursuits?" "How much money, status, or power will they bring me?" (Maslow, p. 164).

The difference between achievers and performers in this regard is that achievers look at work, human encounters, and life situations as potentially fulfilling activities by themselves. Achievers, like performers, prefer challenging contacts, people from whom they can learn; however, they are more willing to say, "Even if I don't 'get' much from this guy, it was interesting to see what he was like. He was a wonderful character." Achievers are more accepting. Performers are more calculating. Performers want to take from their encounters something they can use to get ahead. Achievers are more willing to give something to their human engagements.

Achievers, then, are more problem-solvers than self-protectors or ego-enhancers. They are able to focus on objectives without becoming lost in the means to them as commanders do. To achievers, the key questions are what should be done, what is important, what are the objectives we desire. After formulating goals, they develop the appropriate means for reaching them. Nonachievers select goals according to how well they fit with the means, present location, convenience, protocol, and standardized procedures, rather than how significant the results will be. Nonachievers often lose sight of their original objectives by devoting their lives to the means of reaching them, by measuring how well they follow the rules, and by conforming to rituals instead of measuring how good the outcomes are. Achievers feel, as Maslow so well put it, "What is not worth doing is not worth doing" (Maslow, p. 18).

The ability to focus on problems allows achievers to approach their work boldly and take creative steps to solve challenges. Similarly, they are more realistic and objective about work because they less often distort communications, block out what they do not want to hear, or fearfully ignore relevant information.

Achievers Are Creative

You might think again now of the achievers you know. How creative are they? How innovative are they? The achievers I have studied have proved to be highly creative, inventive, and imaginative. They see things freshly, are able to develop novel thoughts and solutions to problems and invent unique ways of entertaining themselves. Since they are not afraid of the unknown or the confusing, they are able to penetrate into new areas without carrying with them old stereotypes to order their experiences. Rather, they are comfortable with uncertainty. They are able to see events innocently, nonjudgmentally. Abraham Lincoln, for example, demonstrated this talent by his ability to resist great pressures to rush into action, to make premature decisions when he felt the real problems had not been discovered or analyzed.

Achievers judge their own feelings and human situations more accurately than most. Their perceptions are less biased by wishful thinking or ego-building needs. They live in the real world most of the time for they screen out the superficial stereotypes which consume much of our everyday attention. The uncritically open eyes of a child are similar to those of adult achievers, for they do not fear what they might see, do not shy away from the unknown, or prematurely categorize the social cues they receive. They are able to see the unique elements in a situation and thus behave more realistically toward them.

Achievers' lack of inhibition allows them to behave creatively. Dancing or singing, for instance, reflects this trait. Achievers can lose themselves, let themselves go with the beat, the music, the noises and movements. They are able to create spontaneous and unusual steps, rhythms, and movements. Nonachievers are more structured, awkwardly working hard at trying to keep time with the music, to follow the exact notes, to appear natural. Achievers' creativeness displays a lack of artificiality, a natural responsiveness to the cues in their situations.

They Explore Achievers also are explorers. They search their environment for new ideas and means for reaching their objectives. Their high self-confidence allows them to ask questions of themselves such as: "How did I do? Why did that work this way? How do other people do their jobs? Why do my students learn from one style of teaching and not another? Why do some products sell while others don't?" Achievers have an unconscious mechanism which guides them to seek self-improvement and exercise their talents effectively by accepting feedback.

Even achievers' doodles on paper capture the movement, energy, and dynamism of their character. Achievers draw single, unattached straight lines, more S-shaped, diagonal, purposeful lines than do nonachievers who draw fuzzy, overlaid, scribbled, and horizontal lines (McClelland, p. 304).

Achievers Have Deep, Genuine Human Relationships

Because of their self-acceptance, achievers are natural in their relationships. They open their feelings for viewing by others, communicate trust and authenticity; therefore, they instill similar feelings in their associates. Their openness to their inner life minimizes the number of secrets they have and want to keep. Accordingly, they are open more than most to deep, genuine, long-lasting friendships and love relationships.

Indeed, my experience strongly suggests that truly fulfilling marriages seldom occur but when they do they are usually between spouses who are achievers.

A fine-tuned relationship between two humans is an exceedingly fleeting joy to grasp. Unless the individuals are able to remove their defenses to allow their feelings to be exposed, to accept themselves enough so they can care and accept another, they are unlikely to form a mutually enriching, deep, authentic love. I also believe that sexual relationships follow the same principles. Unless unguarded love and the ingredients that precede it exist, it is unlikely that meaningful sexual relationships will prevail.

They Feel Without Fear Achievers, then, have more intense feelings. They have peak experiences, feel high, floating, gleeful from natural events, their work, leisure and friendship, without help from artificial stimulation. They are not ''mechanical men'' who fear to love or to feel because of the pain that might result when their feelings are crushed.

Rollo May suggests, for example, that those who prevent themselves from becoming deeply committed to their children, spouse, or friends fear that the relationship might end by death and that the pain would be over-powering (Rollo May, *Love and Will*, 1969, p. 105). To buffer this pain, they choke off their feelings and become robots in work, sex, leisure, friendships and marriage. They say to themselves, ''If one never feels, he never suffers.'' It is as if one tries to hurry through the things he fears to blur them from his consciousness so that he can get them over with.

They Are Contented By accepting their personal wishes and needs and by being able to perceive their experiences openly, achievers more often than most can see, in the simple everyday patterns of life, the fresh and the beautiful. They are able to sense pleasure in their present existence and do not often feel the itch to find ''greener pastures.'' They see the ''green'' in their own situations, the fortune of their own positions. They realize their spouses, friends, and careers are by nature imperfect, but they feel lucky; indeed, many are amazed at having the things they have.

They Have Compassion Since achievers are not distracted by surface symbols of a person's qualities—color, religion, dress, age, education, money and power—these artificial symbols are placed in the background when they relate to people. They perceive more clearly than most the real person, his genuine beliefs, values, motivations, fears, and meaningful contributions. Achievers look for a person's worth regardless of his outer trimmings. Their commitment to work that centers beyond their own personal needs and their calm, long-term effort to improve the world illustrate their brotherly concern for others. This concern conveys a spirit of compassion, a caring for other people. This also is related to the fact that their relations are close and personal, not superficial, social, "business," or "cocktail" friendships.

Achievers Are Ethical Achievers are strongly ethical, for they have well-developed moral codes and philosophies that guide their lives. Their codes concerning superficial customs might well differ from those of the society in which they live. Yet, they are more ethical than most people. They may not go to church every Sunday, for example, but are often kinder, more caring, fair, and honest than many regular church goers.

Since they are growth-motivated—concerned with reaching their potentials, carrying out their skills and interests on meaningful problems—and are much less deficiency-motivated—striving to raise their self-esteem by performing for others, protecting themselves, hiding, pleasing or controlling others—they are able to withstand pressures to do or say things they do not believe. They have integrity.

Achievers Have Fun A somewhat different reason why many people are attracted to achievers is their ability to genuinely relax, have fun, laugh, and be peaceful with themselves. They want to enjoy life; therefore, they keep their work and other commitments in perspective with their physical and psychological happiness. They display more expressive behavior—laughing, smiling, jumping, stopping to smell a fragrant flower—and less coping or structured behavior than most people.

Their humor fits into their moods and situations. It is not artificially buttressed by a reservoir of hostile or off-color jokes, hidden sarcasm, or unreal laughter. Rather, it is responsive to man's nature or unusual situations (Maslow, p. 161).

Achievers Perform Meaningful and Challenging Jobs Well

Achievers prefer jobs, hobbies, and activities that are challenging as well as meaningful, for they like to exert personal initiative and variety into their work. Adolescent and young adult achievers prefer activities that provide stimulation and visible results. Similarly, older achievers devote their leisure time to hobbies that allow them to reach their potential. They may select photography, scuba diving, golf, tennis, gardening, bird-watching, or wine collecting. However, even if an activity contains all of the ingredients for achievement potential—moderate risks, challenges, chance for self-reliance, and feedback—they will not try to accomplish it if they do not believe in the job. If they think playing bridge is meaningless, for example, even though it might be very challenging, they would probably slough the game, bid poorly, and try to get their partners to play the hands.

When they find the right tasks, achievers experience great personal pleasure from working on and attaining their goals. When teachers evaluated their students on how much they enjoyed different activities, for example, achievers were rated as enjoying accomplishments and doing their work much more than nonachievers. Similarly, when students were placed in homogeneous classes, that is, with other students of equal ability, achievers enjoyed the challenge rather than being panicked by it and performed better than did nonachievers (Atkinson, p. 254).

When offered a better job that would require them to move away from their parents and hometown, achievers are usually willing to move. They are strong enough to leave their parents and community ties for assignments they consider important—those that will allow them to develop their potential. As Fromm suggests, a person cannot become truly mature and independent until he breaks from his parents psychologically. The achiever is able to do this (Eric Fromm, *Man For Himself*, 1947).

They Are Realistic Achievers like jobs which require them to exert themselves fully, yet give them a reasonable chance of succeeding. They ask, ''Why should I spend the time working on jobs where I cannot do well. Why not switch to another activity where I can be more effective?'' They can admit to themselves and others their limitations and strengths.[1]

Achievers dislike activities in which they have little chance of succeeding—a low probability of success, like 10 percent. The recent experience of a $40-million-a-year high technology firm illustrates this point well. For three years, the president and vice-presidents had jointly set realistic, yet challenging goals (50 percent probability of success). Each year the firm had exceeded these goals by 15 to 20 percent. For the fourth year, after the managers had set their goals, the president strongly encouraged them to raise their estimates by 15 percent, since they had gone over their goals in the past. The subordinates disagreed but followed the president's urging.

A top vice-president, an achiever, reported: ''We started out working like hell, but pretty soon began to realize it would be impossible to achieve the 'raised goal.' So, I said to myself, 'I haven't taken a vacation in a long time. I might as well do it this year because we can't reach the goal anyhow.' People just kind of gave up.'' The company fell 30 percent below the goal it had originally set.

Conversely, when achievers are given tasks for which the probability of successful performance is high, they lose interest. As they master old problems, they look for new ones. Achievers love to initiate new projects, but after the creative design work is done and the major problems are solved, they have difficulty following through on the details, for this is generally less risky and less meaningful to them than is the creation of solutions.

Achievers, then, are realistic in setting goals. High school and college students who are achievers, for example, set much more

1. College students were given an exam they had three hours to complete, but few students worked for the full three hours. Achievers, however, stayed much longer than nonachievers. Similarly, Air Force personnel were given a set of complex problems to work on and were allowed to leave whenever they desired. Achievers were willing to stay longer to accomplish the project than nonachievers (Atkinson, p. 244). Supporting this point was a research project done on eleven to twelve-year-old pupils who were given assignments and then interrupted before they completed them. At a later time the students were allowed to resume their activities and to select the tasks they had completed to do again or work on those which were unsolved. Achievers preferred the unsolved assignments much more than did nonachievers. They were persistent in their efforts to satisfy their unfulfilled needs for accomplishment (Heckhausen, p. 109).

challenging yet reasonable occupational and scholarship goals than nonachievers. They seldom have over-aspirations or under-aspirations in relation to their past abilities, intelligence, grades and socioeconomic class (McClelland, p. 336; Heckhausen, p. 108).

Pete Robinson, for example, a fifty-four-year-old businessman had, over a twelve-year period, built a profitable real estate firm in San Francisco. He entered my office feeling bored, tired, and frustrated. After an intense conversation, it was apparent that Pete could continue to lead his firm and personally make over $300,000 a year. Yet he had lost interest in the job. His partner was the inside man—organized, careful, and systematic, a commander. They made a tremendous team. But things were going too well, for Pete no longer felt a challenge. Making $300,000 a year in real estate was like throwing darts at a target from one foot away for Pete. He soon left the operation of his business to his partner and entered a completely different field—franchising tax-accounting services. He moved away from the dart board and made his job more difficult so he could enjoy it more.

It is interesting to apply these ideas to the achiever in sports. Jim Ryun, the track superstar, was the first high schooler to break the four-minute mile. Next, he set a goal to break the existing U.S.A. mile record. After accomplishing this, he raised his goal (to put the probability of success back down to fifty-fifty on his new activity) to be the fastest man in the world. After he succeeded, reporters bombarded him with the question, ''What are you going to do now?'' He replied, ''I'm going to try different distance events.'' He again reached his objective. Subsequently, in the famous race in Florida, Ryun stopped abruptly in the middle of the race, and retired from track for many months. He commented, ''I just lost interest. I couldn't make myself run.'' It might well have been that the activity was becoming too boring for Ryun. But since he quit for many months, he greatly lowered his chance of success and raised the challenge in running. Accordingly, he started competing again.

One cannot help speculating whether this need for a challenge helps to explain why a great athlete at the peak of his career changes occupations. He might quit boxing or football, for example, to become a singer or businessman. Similarly, this might explain why wealthy businessmen accept a meager salary in politics. The achiever's need for fifty-fifty challenges in meaningful tasks at least suggests this possibility.

An achiever like Arnold Palmer, for example, might lose interest in his profession—winning major golf tournaments—because the activity loses its meaning, becomes too easy, and the probability of being excellent at it too high. He then seeks substitute outlets, however, that give him a chance for exercising his skills. In his case, the goals might be success in business entreprenuership.

Achievers do better, then, on tasks that: (1) they feel are important and meaningful; (2) permit learning: (3) demand concentration; (4) provide realistic challenges; (5) allow them to be self-reliant; (6) give honest feedback; and (7) offer successful levels of difficulty.[2]

In my interviews with administrators and executives, I ask them on first meeting to write down the name and a careful description of the behavior of their best and worst subordinate. Overwhelmingly, they describe an achiever as their best subordinate and an avoider or attacker as their worst. Correspondingly, I have asked "Who is the best leader you have ever known?" Again, an achiever is most frequently selected. It must be remembered, of course, that all types of leadership and personality styles can be very effective in a given job. But, in general, achievers seem to be most preferred, especially at higher organizational levels.

Research has also shown that achievers move up in socioeconomic class more frequently than nonachievers (Crockett). Similarly, most college students score higher on need for achievement than noncollege students, even when the IQ factor is neutralized. They get better grades and drop out of school less frequently than nonachievers do (Atkinson, p. 255). Also, boys from lower social

---

2. For instance, fifteen-year-old achievers who were given three weeks of programmed instruction did progressively better than nonachievers. They had a chance to improve and to learn and worked to do so (Heckhausen, pp. 154–160). Individuals high on achievement also perform better on arithmetic and verbal tasks than low achievers (Atkinson, p. 232). When achievers are placed in homogeneous class groupings, that is, with other students of similar abilities, they perform better than when they are in a class with highly mixed skills (Atkinson, p. 255).

classes who have high needs for achievement make it to the top schools much more frequently than do low achievers (Gerald Bell, *Social Forces*, 1963).

Studies of American executives indicate that achievers get paid more and promoted faster than nonachievers. This relationship was not as strong, however, in government organizations. In government, higher-ranking officials had only a slightly greater achievement need than lower level officials (McClelland, p. 270).

In a careful analysis of the economic growth of different countries, David McClelland has shown that societies with high needs for achievement have much higher rates of economic growth than do low-achievement countries.[3] The United States and Japan, with fast-growing economies, scored high on the achievement factor, while many South American countries, with more stagnant economies, scored low (McClelland).

Preliterate societies with high achievement needs had more entrepreneurial activities and more advanced complex technologies. During the great growth period in ancient Greece, the achievement factor was at its highest among the Greeks. After this peak, the achievement factor decreased and the society declined (McClelland, p. 107).

Achievers Develop Intelligence

Evidence suggests that achievers have high IQ than low achievers. Since achiever parents give their children independence, responsibility, feedback about their behavior, reinforcement for accomplishments, much stimulation and encouragement to explore their environment, they have a variety of experiences which they learn to evaluate carefully. These seem to aid the development of intelligence.[4]

3. It is likely, however, that McClelland's measures combined achiever and performer personality types.

4. Research suggests, for instance, that there is a significant correlation between IQ and need for achievement in high IQ groups. That is, if you select out of a group those who have the highest IQ's, you find that these individuals also rank at the top on achievement motivation. An interesting parallel is found for Air Force recruits with high intelligence. Those highest in IQ scored highest on achievement motivation. Similar findings have been discovered for eleven-and twelve-year-old children and for students in the third grade (Heckhausen, p. 138).

One study reveals that six-year-old children who have high needs for achievement have a significantly greater increase in their IQ's by the time they grow to be teenagers than other youngsters. Probably, these findings partially occur because intelligence encourages individuals to explore, to seek excellence, to increase their achievement needs; and partially because the need for achievement encourages a person to learn to grow and to acquire critical abilities. Intelligence and achievement feed each other (Heckhausen, p. 138).

Achievers Are 100 Percent Psychologically Healthy

Achievers are very psychologically healthy. They have a genuine, positive feeling about themselves. They like themselves, feel contented with their place in life, accept their strengths and weaknesses. They are quite self-contained, for they rely on their own values for deciding their lives, follow their feelings, and trust their judgment.

Genuine satisfaction with who they are allows them to search for even greater depths of personal fulfillment and maturity. Consequently, they react spontaneously to their emotions and guide their own lives without being manipulated by prestige, career or friendship pressures. Relaxation, sleep, and consuming joy come easily and often for them. Seldom do strains of fear, anxiety, or guilt paralyze achievers as compared to the other five personality types, for achievers experience more genuine happiness in living. For these reasons, I rank achievers 100 percent psychologically healthy. They are, of course, not perfect. But they come closest to reaching the maximum *human potential* for personal fulfillment. A description of what I consider to be psychologically healthy human beings is provided in this entire chapter on the achiever, for he, in my judgment, represents the best that we as human animals can become.

Achievers' weaknesses are that they sometimes become impatient with others for imposing their personality needs on them. They sometimes ignore others since they need them less than most. Similarly, they can upset people with their spontaneous outbursts of pleasure or anger, and their lack of inhibitions occasionally upset others who are less spontaneous.

SUMMARY

How far are you from being an achiever? Who do you know well who comes closest to being an achiever? I have discovered one problem people have in answering this question is that they do not know many people very well; thus, they cannot judge them thoroughly. If this is true for you, you might try over the next few weeks to get to know very well several people you think are achievers so you can try these ideas out. Talk to them, ask them about their lives, their goals. Try to understand them.

To help you in your own growth, see how many of the eleven major characteristics of the achiever you can summarize below.

1. Spontaneous / Natural
2. High Self Confidence
3. Self Reliant
4. Goal Oriented
5. Problem - centered
6. Creative
7. Genuine Human Relations
8. Perform Meaningful & Challenging Jobs Well
9. Develop Intelligence
10. Environment Warmth Increases Independence
11. 100 % Psychologically Healthy

PART II

CHAPTER 8

How to Apply
the Six Types of Personality

What difference does it make whether you understand people's psychological needs? If you understand personality, it means you can work with people more effectively, enjoy them more creatively, and enhance your own psychological health. The purpose of part II is to provide you with methods for applying to your life the concepts discussed in the first section of this book. The major focus is upon how each of the six types of persons acts out his needs as a leader of people. Specifically, I examine how each personality style manages or relates to others.

Why study leadership styles to learn how to apply your understanding of motivation? Because you spend most of your time leading or relating to others. Thus, part II is aimed at the most pervasive part of your life—how you relate to people.

What Is Leadership Style?

Your style of leadership consists of your habits, work patterns, and stable mannerisms you use to manage or to relate to others. The way you influence people to do things is your individual leadership style. Leadership style is the same thing as your management, administrative, coaching, teaching, or parental training style. Consequently, for all situations in which you have a formal or informal position of authority, i.e., the ability to influence others' behavior,

I will use the term *leadership style* to refer to your ways of influencing others.

Your style of leadership can be divided into five major dimensions. They are: (1) goal-setting, (2) decision-making, (3) feedback, (4) conflict resolution, and (5) empacation. Empacation is a word I invented to refer to interpersonal communications, listening, trust, support, and empathy.

Goal-Setting When leading others, you determine your subordinate's goals. You communicate, either explicitly or implicitly, and in varying amounts, what you expect from them. The goals you establish vary as to (1) how much risk they entail, (2) how clear they are, (3) how much detail is included, and (4) how much they coincide with your superior's objectives.[1]

Decision-Making As a leader you make decisions that affect your subordinates and associates. Your decision-making style varies according to (1) how thoroughly you accept your decision-making responsibility, (2) the initiatives you take for selecting alternatives and (3) how much participation you seek from subordinates.

Feedback on Performance Subordinates perform their jobs with different degrees of success. You judge their performance and then tell them your evaluation. The type of feedback on performance you give and receive varies as to how thoroughly, clearly, accurately, constructively, and frequently it is given.

Conflict Resolution Your style of reacting to conflict influences your leadership effectiveness significantly. You have an individualistic style of behaving when in conflict with others. When angered, you express it. Your expression may be immediate and direct or delayed and indirect. Many times after leaving an argument, for example, you think of stinging points you could have made. Your anger is still coming out.

Similarly, you might release your anger on the golf course by swinging your club so vigorously that you shake the earth, or play

---

1. Other terms that are used frequently to refer to the goal-setting dimensions of leadership are directing, initiating, structuring, and planning.

tennis violently because you would rather hit the ball hard to release your hostilities than to hit the ball well to win points.

Your response to conflicts can be divided into the following dimensions: the degree to which you confront them directly, prevent them from occurring, accept compromises rather than final solutions, assign blame for their occurrence, and approach the sources of the conflicts directly rather than through a third party.

Empacation Empacation refers to your skills in empathy and communication. We do not have a word in our language which accurately refers to the concept of skills in *interpersonal relationships*. Since it is such an important factor in our lives, it deserves a specific name. Therefore, I have combined *empathy* (the ability to feel another's situation) and *communication* (the direct exchange of ideas with others) to produce the word empacation. I use empacation to define the degree to which you: (1) *communicate* your feelings, beliefs and ideas completely; (2) *listen* carefully without blocking, turning out, or thinking of quick one-upmanship responses; (3) *show confidence*, warmth, and support toward others (*as indicated by your manner of expressing humor*); (4) *show acceptance* instead of hostility or aggression toward others as indicated by your temper; (5) *act nondefensively* as indicated by the degree and intensity of your openness and trust in your relationship, and (6) *sense* the feelings, attitudes, and reactions of others—act empathetically.

You Have a Mixture of These Styles

Each of the six personality types carries out his leadership role in a unique style according to his personality characteristics. Thus, we can label six styles of leadership.

You should remember that the six styles of leadership we are discussing, like the personality types, are pure types—the classical models of leadership. Most people do not fit cleanly into a pure type, but are a mixture of these models.

Your Leadership Style Is Similar to Your Relationship Style

It is significant for you to understand completely the following point: the way in which you lead others is almost the same as the way in which you relate to others. The way you relate to your spouse, raise your child, coach your team, associate with your friends, get along with your relatives, parents, neighbors, fraternity brothers or sorority sisters, requires from you almost identical behavior as being a formal leader or manager. The main difference is that, on the job, your relationships are more formal.

Why is this so significant? Because the ideas I present about leadership apply directly to your style of relating to others. This is strikingly apparent when you examine how you behave with your spouse, children, or friends, for example. When you interact with them, you expect things from them (goal-setting). When you are doing things with them, you decide alternatives regarding them (decision-making). When they do something you do not like, you evaluate their behavior and usually express it in some form (feedback). When you have a fight with them, you resolve your differences in some manner (conflict resolution). You communicate intimately and constantly with them (empacation).

As you see, these everyday processes of living with others are basically the same ones you exhibit in leadership roles. There are three important conclusions to draw from this fact. (1) You can examine your own *leadership* or *relationship style* even if you are not now in a leadership position in a formal organization. If you are a housewife, student, physician, or self-employed individual, you can apply the following ideas to your interpersonal relationships. (2) Similarly, if you are a parent, you can explore how to relate to and lead your children and spouse. (3) Since your behavior in an administrative position is similar to how you act toward others in your everyday relationships—you carry your personality needs around with you from situation to situation and try to satisfy your major needs wherever you can—you can improve your work associations and private relationships by studying the following ideas about leadership.

Try to apply the discussions about leadership to your relationships. Ask yourself, "How do I relate to others?" "How do I react to conflicts?" "How close do I get to people?" "How critical of others am I?" "How do I coach my children?"

Part II explores the leadership characteristics of the six personality models by examining the consequences of each style for both productivity and personal satisfaction. It also shows what kind of situations each style functions most and least effectively in; the type of people each style works best and worst with; how to get along most effectively with a person of each style; how best to change each style; and finally, how to use these concepts to improve the social, economic and psychological environment we live in.

Chapter 9 begins with an examination of the above issues for the commander. The remaining chapters concentrate on the other five styles.

The Commander's Leadership Style

The commander's leadership style is easy to recognize because his actions are highly visible and consistent. When you meet him, he strikes you forcefully, leaving an indelible mark upon your senses, which does not allow you to forget him readily.

Frequently, I ask a manager to describe his work associates. When he begins to tell me about the commander, I stop him and say, "Is he like . . ." and I give him a portrait of a commander leader. In startled response, the manager asks, "When did you meet him?" So consistent is the commander's style of leadership that he is the most well-informed, easily-grasped type of the six styles of leadership.

Goal Setting

The commanders I have studied set high, difficult goals for themselves and their subordinates. Although they usually involve little risk, their goals demand strenuous effort. If a commander is a football coach, for instance, his players must strain their physical resources to accomplish his wishes, but they seldom need to master complex or varied plays. Their goals require more effort than creativity, more discipline than risk.

Commanders stress the means to their goals as much as the final objectives. In fact, often they lose sight of their primary goals by becoming enamored with the methods for reaching them. They forget that their objectives are to make a profit or to win the game, for example, because they concentrate so deeply on discipline and order.

Decision Making

Commander leaders make decisions for their subordinates. They seldom seek advice or listen to their opinions. They gather much information through reports and studies, but seldom engage their people in active participation. Once they make a decision, it is firm. Since they dislike subordinates who question them, subordinates learn to keep their thoughts to themselves.

Feedback on Performances

Commanders, I have observed, give much feedback, especially when subordinates deviate from their directives. If their subordinates do a good job, they give them some positive feedback, but then imply "Remember, this is why we are paying you." They expect perfection without rewarding it. They keenly sense insubordination and punish it. This makes their subordinates fearful of their jobs, and consequently, eager to follow their orders. Subordinates feel they have little chance to improve, so they had better do things right—the commander's way—the first time!

Conflict Resolution

Commander leaders cut off conflicts abruptly for they find them upsetting. They arbitrarily decide what they think is the proper solution. Because they do not seek to resolve conflicts by mutual discussion, they cause their subordinates to suppress a great deal of anger. Subordinates do not deal with their tensions, they merely hide them. Creativity is stifled, and open communication is smothered. Subordinates of commanders, then, often redirect their pent-up frustrations toward each other instead of toward their commander leaders. When things are going poorly, their anxieties often explode.

Empacation

Commanders' empacation skills can be divided into the following dimensions:

Communications   Commanders are one-way communicators. Their subordinates say, "He is a difficult guy to get to know, because he doesn't reveal his beliefs. He is a private person. He tells you what to do. He talks about getting the product out, but that's it."

Listening   Commanders hear what they want to hear, then dominate the conversation by stating what they think is right and how the subordinate's idea is wrong.

Supportiveness   The commander leaders' support of their work associates, as revealed by their humor, is stiff and awkward. Seldom do they tell friendly jokes which show confidence. This somewhat "standoffish" attitude caused one subordinate of a commander to say, "I feel uptight around him, like I shouldn't smile." Indeed, it is interesting to try to imagine someone like Charles de Gaulle, a good example of a commander leader, being overcome with spontaneous laughter. It is easier to envision his dry, distilled humor.

Hostility—Temper   Having a violent temper, commanders often nourish conflict among their subordinates by releasing their negative feelings upon them. Correspondingly, their own anxieties build because they do not resolve problems they have with others or explore their own feelings in regard to them.
    Think, for example, of a commander you know and ask, "When does he get angry? What causes it?" Typically, you find he loses his temper when subordinates defy him or things become unpredictable—when he loses absolute control. Seldom does he work problems out; rather he steams inside until he explodes.

Defensiveness   Commander leaders are moderately defensive. They are candid in criticizing subordinates; however, they are not open when looking at their own motivations. Their personal likes, feelings, ambitions, loves, and softer emotions are their own, well-kept secrets. Thus, they hide them behind defensive shields.

Sensitivity—Empathy Those commander leaders I have examined have great difficulty perceiving others' feelings. Since they have little need to please or to impress, they have little motivation to learn about people so they can manage them effectively. Because their primary need is for structure, they view emotions as interfering with their control; thus, they eliminate feelings from the job. They are insensitive, cold, and unyielding. They mean well, but come across as a rock-like personality.

Where Do Commanders Fit?

Best-Fit Situations The commander leads best within the job that is confronted by stable *environmental* forces, requires performance of clear-cut *tasks*, and operates within an *organizational* structure that is orderly and precise—the commander organizational system. Examples are mass production, automobile assembly lines, textile, systems, manufacturing, bank operations, computer and accounting services, and the military. Generally, in these situations, he rigidly asserts his control, dominates the routines and those who perform them, and concentrates on the means to the ends. He doesn't have to worry much about the ultimate goals since they change less frequently than in more complex organizational systems. His rigid leadership style matches the rigid demands of the situation. This match creates effectiveness. This is his best-fit-adjustment situation.

Worst-Fit Situations When the environmental pressures, technology, and organizational structure in which the commander works are flexible, dynamic, unpredictable, and complex (the Achievement Organizational System), he performs worst. His leadership style conflicts directly with demands for changing, creative solutions, candid, intimate communications, and constant adaptability to unique problems.[1]

Best-Matched People The commander works most effectively with the avoider, for the avoider enjoys being controlled and relishes

---

1. The commander produces average results in organizational systems that come in between the commander and the achiever systems.

following details. The avoider's meekness, in turn, reinforces the commander's power. If a head football coach is a commander, for example, he gets along best with assistant coaches and players who are avoiders. Similarly, the commander-husband desires an avoider wife; the commander-teacher prefers avoider students.[2]

Worst-Matched People The commander has the most difficulty dealing with the achiever. The achiever is unpredictable, changing, and spontaneous. These traits smack the commander in the face, for they directly oppose what the commander needs. The commander prefers order, but gets ambiguity from the achiever. He prefers aloof relationships, but is offered warm associations by the achiever. He prefers subservience from others, but is faced with self-reliance from the achiever. For these reasons, their relationship is stormy and mutually distasteful.

General Consequences of the Commander's Style of Leadership

When the types of people and work situations in which a commander leads are not rigid, but are a mixture of types of people and situations, the commander is less effective. The general consequences of his style of leadership in mixed situations are as follows.

Efficiency In almost all situations, he is strikingly well-organized, detailed, systematic, disciplined and efficient. Things are done on time. Everyone knows what, when, how and where he should perform. Indeed, running an efficient organization is the commander's strong suit.

Morale Because he is rigidly demanding, the commander smothers his associates. He crushes their feelings and suppresses their initiative. Consequently, his subordinates are usually dissatisfied. Turnover, absenteeism, and accidents flourish under his tutelage, reflecting the dissatisfaction.

2. The commander gets along moderately well with the other four personality types, but he has rather poor relations with the attacker, because the attacker defies him.

Personal Growth   Similarly, the self-development of his subordinates is stunted by the commander's autocratic rule. He rewards those who cause few problems, silently follow his directives, and stick to routines. He punishes those who create unexpected events, ask questions, or deviate from his policies. Subordinates' opportunities for improvement are severely restricted, then, in the commander's domain. His subordinates often lack experience and motivation to be promoted because they are trained for incapacity. Other divisions within an organization seldom look to his department to find key management talent.[3]

Organizational Growth   The commander's organization is inflexible and resistant to change. Consequently, new environmental forces are often ignored. Two years ago, I noticed an article, hidden in the middle of a small southern newspaper, which reported the closing of a textile corporation after sixty years of business. In the 1930s, it had been the largest textile firm in the world. Curiosity led me to the company's door, where I inquired about what had happened. The answer was relatively simple. The firm had been run by a series of commanders. Their method of doing business had not changed in thirty years. The world had left them behind.

By contrast, the Burlington Industries textile firm got started around 1930, and has grown to be one of the largest businesses in the world because it changed, adapted, listened, and responded to the environmental, social, and economic pressures that surrounded it.

The commander's organization, then, is often unresponsive, lacks creativity, and maladapts to environmental pressures.[4]

Overall Effectiveness   Four factors combine to make the commander's total effectiveness *slightly above average*. His (1) efficiency, and (2) forcefulness increase his effectiveness. Yet, his (3) lack of creativity and responsiveness, as well as (4) his poor "people re-

---

3. Leaders in commander organizational systems will, of course, seek his people for they have been trained to fit into a well-oiled machine.
4. This is not to imply that they did not have some rigid individuals within their firm who were extremely strong, driving forces who may have prevented even more effective long-term growth.

lations'' decrease his output. In a mixed job situation, he generally produces more than the avoider, pleaser, and attacker, but less than the performer and achiever. (In a commander organizational system, he produces the highest results.) He climbs to high levels within organizations, but is often blocked from the top positions because of his rigid behavior and poor empacation skills. Top positions typically require much more flexibility and creativity than he possesses.

How Can You Best Get Along With the Commander-Leader?

As his Subordinate   To gain the commander's approval in the shortrun, without trying to change him, the most effective style of behavior is simply to be an avoider. Do what he says, when he wants you to, making sure to follow his instructions to the letter. Do not offer criticism and he will value you highly, as long as you get the work out by following his commands. The other leaders in the organization may not respect you, but the commander will.

As his Superior   Management of the commander is more difficult. You must provide clear directions, emphasize details, yet allow him freedom to implement them. You must be firm and unchanging without taking away his ability to dominate his subordinates. Tell him what to do, then leave him alone. When he is finished, reward him for an efficient job. Make sure to be on call for his frequent questions to clarify details.

As his Peer   To be a successful associate of the commander in his eyes, without trying to change him, you should relate to him in much the same way as his subordinate—be well-organized and passive. The more you behave like an avoider, the more he will like you.

How Can the Commander Change?

Personality change is a complex subtle process. It takes time, energy and much skill. While attempting to change, you often suffer great anxiety because it is not easy to alter the way you are. You must ask yourself: "Is the pain worth the effort?" The answer is up to you. I believe if you approach change realistically and patiently, the results are worth the effort. You do not eliminate your weaknesses by trying to forget them. You live with your problems whether or not you acknowledge them. In my judgment you might as well take a constructive, healthy approach toward personality growth, because this is your major means to reach happiness in your life and to gain self-fulfillment and effectiveness in your work.

The first requirement for change is that you must genuinely want to change. Unless you truly desire to reach new goals, you will not do so.

If you want to change, how do you go about it? If you are a commander and want to become more of an achiever, what should you do? There are five key strategies to change, five rules to follow to help you in your endeavors. These steps are aids to use to begin to change. It will take much time and effort on your part. But you can change. You can be more fulfilled and effective.[5]

Strategy 1: Practice Being Submissive and Equal With Others   Since you are a commander, you must learn to relate to others, at times, submissively and, more often, equally. You should consciously take a dependent position when the situation is appropriate. You should ask others to take the lead so you can practice following. Similarly, you should seek equal give-and-take in discussions. By asking another individual for his opinion and fully listening to it, by not mowing him down with your own thoughts, you will taste the pleasures of a more equal, open relationship. You will also be surprised how much you learn from other people.

Strategy 2: Practice Seeing Both Sides of the Story   To overcome your categorical thinking and stereotyped beliefs, you should list your stereotypes, then try to be your own worst critic by finding as many faults with them as you can. Catch yourself when you make a categorical conclusion, and practice seeing as many aspects of the topic as you can. If you say that all young people are not

---

5. If you are a commander and want to remain so, to enhance your commander needs merely seek out your best-fit-situation—a commander environment.

good, for example, ask, "What are their good points and bad points?" "Under what conditions are they good and bad?" "Why do I feel the way I do" Try finding fresh ideas by challenging your old beliefs.

Strategy 3: Practice Being Less Organized and More Spontaneous
To loosen up your tight self-discipline, design certain times when you have no plans, goals, rules or things to do. Let yourself react naturally to the situations you encounter. Spontaneously follow your impulses, making sure to avoid your standard activities and routines. Let your desk get messy for a whole day, for example. You need not worry about becoming too disorganized, for you have too far to travel for that to happen.

Strategy 4: Get Involved in Unstructured Situations Instead of automatically choosing jobs, assignments, friends, or activities that serve your needs for structure, seek situations that are flexible, confusing, and unclear. Make a special effort to enter an environment that is unpredictable, then, examine how you react. Expose yourself to newness. Learn how to adapt to change by accepting variety as a positive goal, rather than as something to be shunned.

Strategy 5: Practice Being Warm and Intimate with Others. To develop your "people skills" and to overcome your aloofness, make a conscious effort to get to know several individuals very well. Open yourself up for friendship by being warm and honest about your feelings, personal beliefs, and attitudes. Hold firm when the impulse grabs you to fly away from a relationship. Stand up to your feelings. Ask other people what their feelings are. Try to put yourself in their shoes to determine their feelings.

How Do You Get the Commander to Want to Change?

What do you do if the commander does not want to change? What if he does not want to try the five strategies listed previously? How can you create within him the desire to reach higher levels of psychological health and effectiveness?

If you want to instill the desire in the commander to become more of an achiever, for example—to be more self-reliant, self-confident, secure, spontaneous, honest, and realistic, willing to explore, able to trust his own judgment—my experience suggests six steps.

Six Key Steps to Create Change

Step One The first step is to honestly accept him as he is without passing judgment, ridiculing, manipulating, tricking, overpraising, attacking or lying to him. If you can truly accept him for what he is, if you can value him as a human being with imperfections, as we all have, then you can listen to him in such a manner that he feels you will not harm him. He will not worry about losing face but will concentrate on understanding his weaknesses so he can improve. In a sense, by accepting him in a nonevaluative manner, you act as a human mirror in which he can see himself. You ask questions, listen, and try to understand. Consequently, in your reflective questioning, in your efforts to understand him, he will learn about himself.

Step Two By accepting the commander, you will make him feel secure and unthreatened. Therefore, he will lower his defenses enough to peer beneath the surface of his inner self. To open his feelings for study, he risks personal failure. You must help him realize that the long-run gains outweigh the short-run risks. To do this, you must make him feel psychologically safe. He must trust you. You gain his trust by accepting him.

Step Three By making the commander feel unthreatened, he will begin to conduct research on himself. You must stimulate him to study himself carefully, to take time to analyze his actions, to compare his behavior with others, to ask how others are reacting to him, to make use of his feelings by letting them guide him to an understanding of his true motivations. You must encourage him to conduct self-research.

Step Four His self-research will lead him to a more careful understanding of his personality needs. To determine how far he has to go, he must know where he is starting from. For the commander to change, he must come to terms with himself. Otherwise, he will resist feedback, hide from his own weaknesses, and avoid new forms of behavior. Since he is the one who is going to change, he must understand why. You must help him understand himself.

Step Five After he understands who he is, you must encourage the commander to set goals, to establish ideal targets to shoot for. He must decide which weaknesses he wants to remove and which traits he desires to develop. He must know where he is going in order to get there. If he wants to become more of an achiever, for instance, he must understand fully the characteristics of the achiever. Then he must practice acting like that which he wants to become.

Step Six You must motivate the commander to take actions to change, to take some risks, to accept occasional failure, and to experiment with alternative forms of behavior. He must want to change. He must want to become an achiever. You must urge him to actively try to change. In order to fly, he must practice.

In implementing these six key steps, if you succeed in step one, then step two will follow. If you do step two, then step three results, and so forth because these steps are cumulative. One must be accomplished for the next to follow.

Also, it helps in accepting others in the manner described in step one if you are an achiever, for it takes a great deal of self-confidence to accept someone who is different from you. If you lack self-esteem, when someone disagrees with you, you typically feel threatened and think you might be the one who is wrong. If you can degrade him sufficiently, you raise your position, and thus bolster your weakly-held self-confidence. So try to work on your own self-confidence when you try step one.

The application of the six key steps toward creating change in the commander has unique demands because of his personality qualities. You must be direct and quite structured during the first phases of your efforts to change him. You must tell him what you would like to do, why, when, and how. You cannot be passive and completely nondirective at first, for this is too great a contrast with his best-fit-situational preferences. It is like throwing him into freezing water. You have to coach him away gradually from his structured style. You must remove your initial structured approach step by step, according to his ability to stand by himself. As he gets used to the water, you can become more nondirective.

SUMMARY

To help you master your understanding of the commander leader, see how well you can recall the following topics:

1. What are the basic characteristics of the commander's leadership style? *Difficult Goals / makes Decisions for Subs / Give much Feedback / cutoff conflicts*

2. In which situations does he fit best? *Stable enviro forces*

3. What are the general consequences of his leadership practices?

4. How do you best get along with the commander? *Avoid*

5. How can the commander change? *yes - Is the pain worth the effort*

6. How can you motivate the commander to desire to change?

See pg 139

6 steps

CHAPTER 10

The Attacker's Leadership Style

Attacker leaders I have studied as parents, coaches, teachers, or administrators, find the duties of leadership distasteful, for these duties make them dependent. It is painful for attacker-leaders to report their actions, implement others' plans, keep their bosses informed, and be accountable.

Many attackers end up, nevertheless, in managerial roles. Some inherit positions of leadership. Others mistakenly become entangled in administration, not anticipating the difficulties they will encounter in acting out their needs. After arriving in management posts, I have found that attackers usually ignore the organization's expectations and modify the job to fit their needs. They take little responsibility for their subordinates, preferring to let them struggle for themselves.

Goal Setting

Attacker leaders defy authority by setting goals which oppose accepted policies. The degree of difficulty of their goals is inconsistent because their goals vary according to those set by their bosses. They would rather establish objectives which defy their superiors than worry about how challenging or important they are. Setting goals forces attackers to accept responsibilities. They dislike this. Consequently, attackers confuse goal-setting discussions by picking at definitions, debating the clarity of arguments and ridiculing others' suggestions.

Decision Making

Attacker leaders, somewhat like avoiders, dislike making decisions. When they must do so, they gather their subordinates, dominate the discussions, and criticize their theories. By a process of elimination, the attackers' plans are the only ones left.

Since attackers think their subordinates are against them and not to be trusted, they ignore their subordinates' suggestions. Because of a lack of participation, attackers decisions are arbitrary, inconsistent, and often inaccurate. This erratic decision making behavior gives their subordinates few stable guidelines to follow, for they seldom know what the attacker leaders want next.

Feedback on Performance

Attackers give mostly negative feedback to their subordinates. As one worker described his attacker leader to me, "He has an automatic negative reflex to whatever he sees. If I ask him to evaluate my performance, he ridicules me for asking. If I do not ask, he disparages me for not asking. You just can't do anything right for him."

Conflict Resolution

The attacker leaders I have examined create much conflict because they degrade their associates. Finding a bitter exchange of words enjoyable, they often add to difficulties once they exist. If their subordinates' conflicts become too intensive, however, the attackers are placed in the risky position of having to solve them. To prevent this possibility, they force solutions on their subordinates by shaming them until they swallow their complaints and go on with their work.

Empacation

Communications   Attacker leaders communicate mostly about things that are wrong. They enjoy tearing down popular managers and customs. They coldly ignore their subordinates' feelings and disregard their personal lives. Once they place an individual on their black list, they hold their grudges beyond reason.

Listening   The attacker leaders, in my observations, are poor listeners. They listen to find weaknesses in their subordinates' communications so they can assault them. Understanding their subordinates' positions is not their goal; rather, their purpose is to upset their subordinates' discussions. They frequently interrupt, laugh rudely, and stir up frustrations.

Supportiveness—Humor   Attackers do not show support for their subordinates. If a subordinate makes a mistake or feels upset, they do not sympathize, but instead ridicule him for "being so stupid." Their humor is sarcastic and degrading.

Hostility—Temper   I have observed that attacker-leaders angrily communicate to their subordinates that they feel they are incompetent and lack motivation to do their work well. This crushes their self-esteem causing them to return hostility to the attacker leaders. When the attackers receive their aggression, however, they say to themselves, "Yes, I was right. They are out to do as little as they can and to get me. So I'm going to get them first. The only thing they understand is fear, so I'm going to threaten them plenty." A vicious cycle has begun.

When a brilliant, scholarly, thirty-four-year-old history professor at a large midwestern university was asked by a member of the search committee who was seeking a new president what his strengths and weaknesses were, he retorted: "I don't have to answer that question. It's up to you to sell me, damn it! I'm not a product." One person who knew him commented, "His natural tendency is to explode with bold penetrating strokes. It almost seems like everything he says is calculated to offend."

Defensiveness Attacker managers are defensive. Most subordinates realize if they criticize them, they are likely to receive a bitter comeback from an expert; therefore, many of them hesitate to give feedback to attackers. Attackers overreact to their work associates' questions and take things personally. When one attacker, for example, was asked by his subordinate why he was starting a new project, the attacker replied, "Now you are starting to act like a fool! It is obvious to anyone with sense!"

Sensitivity—Empathy Attacker leaders are moderately skillful in anticipating their subordinates' feelings, but they use their information to hurt rather than to help. They explore how others feel, but only to keep themselves out of trouble.

Where Do Attackers Fit?

Best-Fit Situations When the events and people with whom attackers must deal are themselves negative and aggressive—a hostile environment—attackers cope with them successfully. They adjust to hostility easily for they love competitive battles. Jobs that call for skills in critical evaluation, discovery of weaknesses, and resistance to persuasion (a critical technology) are ones in which attackers perform well.

If the organization design is too controlling, however, attacker leaders are prevented from defying standard procedures. They perform more effectively, therefore, in a loose structure. The freedom to decide how to carry out their jobs lowers their fear of dependence and consequently releases their energies toward self-directed pursuits.

Worst-Fit Situations Attackers perform worst in what can be called a pleaser situation. When the situation requires good public relations, smoothing over conflicts, kind listening with little action, and short-term, superficial contacts, attackers fall flat. Receptionists, airline ticket agents, and secretarial jobs are examples of those in which attackers fit the worst.

Best-Matched People   Attackers I have analyzed work best with bosses, spouses, students, teachers, players, children, peers, and subordinates who are also attackers, for they provide each other a good battle. They reinforce each other's needs and complement their leadership styles by being defiant and hostile. They are mutually independent and competitive, thus they enjoy each other greatly.

Worst-Matched People   Attackers are most upset by pleasers, for pleasers exemplify what they are not: tender and considerate. Consequently, when attackers strike pleasers, it is as if they are hitting pillows. Pleasers give them no feeling of accomplishment. Attackers are frustrated because they cannot act out their needs to assault. Attackers prefer to fight with those who will engage in battle with them. They do not like those who make them feel guilty about their own actions.[1]

Attackers relate with the other four leadership types moderately well, except that they have particular difficulties with commanders. Each time commanders attempt to dominate attackers, they violate directly attackers' major needs for independence. Attackers respond by defying commanders, which in turn frustrates commanders' major needs for control. They get along poorly.

General Consequences of Attackers' Style of Leadership

When attackers are placed in leadership positions that have a mixture of types of people and situations, the general results of their efforts are as follows.

Efficiency   Sporadic efficiency characterizes attackers' operations when they lead in a mixed type of situation. Since they jump impulsively from project to project, they often leave things undone. They wade into a task with full force, stir up great excitement, then dart off to new pursuits. Their short-term, myopic intensity produces long-term inefficiency.

---

1. In short-term contacts attackers prefer to abuse pleasers for they can demonstrate their independence publicly.

Morale   The morale of attackers' subordinates is depressed. Attackers degrade their subordinates, highlight their weaknesses, and ignore their strengths. Subordinates work under constant tensions and fear, hoping to leave when the opportunity appears. They generally hate their attacker leader.

Personal Growth   Personal growth is stifled by the attackers' cynical whips. Attackers' disparaging tongues damage their subordinates' self-confidence. Attackers tear apart their ideas and ridicule their suggestions. They, therefore, become defensive and rebel against the attacker leaders. Rather than searching for ways to improve or for new ideas from which they can grow, subordinates of attackers seek ammunition to use to counterattack.

Organizational Growth   Instead of growing, attackers' organizations typically die. Attacker leaders do not seek effective adaptation to their environments. They do not attempt to stay attuned to the societal changes that occur. Instead, they fight against the situations they encounter rather than cooperate with them.

Overall Effectiveness   When attacker leaders are "turned on" to a project, they pressure their subordinates to get the job done. If the project is constructive and short-run, they are generally effective. The problem, however, is that often they select tasks that have little significance to the organization. Also, they produce better results when working by themselves—in tough sales jobs, for example—than by getting things done through others. Their poor relationships and spotty directions generally do not produce effective work teams.

How Can You Best Get Along With the Attacker-Leader?

As his Subordinate   The most effective short-run way to get along best as an attacker's subordinate is to be an attacker yourself. You should abuse him, fight back when he assaults you and engage in active banter to keep him on his toes. Yet, you should not try to control or restrict his behavior. Let him roam where he desires. He will like you for this.

As his Superior To manage the attacker successfully in the short-run, without trying to change him, you too should behave as an attacker. You should join with him in criticizing others and disparaging the organization, yet encourage him constantly to get his work done.

In addition, you must evaluate his projects carefully to make sure they are important and that he completes them. You must communicate frequently with his subordinates, however, to help relieve the aggression the attacker creates.

As his Peer By behaving as an attacker, you will get along as well as possible with the attacker.

How Can the Attacker Change?

If you are an attacker and want to become more of an achiever, how do you do it? What rules can you follow to make steps toward personal growth? My experience in changing attackers suggests six major strategies you can follow to begin to develop achiever qualities.[2]

Strategy 1: Practice Agreeing Instead of automatically defying authorities and ridiculing standards, try to agree with them. Go along with your boss even though you feel like blasting him. Listen to what others are saying to you. Go along with your family when they hint they would like to do something you typically resist. Try being overly cooperative, just to experience what it is like, for you will discover many insights about yourself. Imagine yourself being cooperative. Picture yourself being happy. Then experience being agreeable.

Strategy 2: Practice Taking Responsibility Seek out responsibility for several specific assignments. Make it visible to your boss, col-

---

2. If you want to enhance your attacker needs then seek out an attacker environment.

leagues, and subordinates that you have done so. Do not hide your commitments. Take on these obligations directly and do your best to stick with them until they are completed. Resist your temptation to escape into new assignments. Finish what you start.

Similarly, when you make a mistake, acknowledge it. Admit your errors and weaknesses, then try to solve them. Practice being honest with yourself and others about your skills and weaknesses. Take responsibility for your actions instead of placing the blame on others.

Strategy 3: Practice Being Constructive Catch yourself tearing down someone's idea; try to build onto it instead. Rather than kill a plan, try to create new and better solutions by adding to it. When you feel the urge to break up a positive relationship between two of your friends or work associates, stop and figure out how you can enhance it. Practice being constructive instead of destructive.

Strategy 4: Practice Being Warm and Friendly To develop your "people skills" and to overcome your harshness, select several individuals, non-attackers, to become good friends with. Make a special effort to be positive, warm, kind, friendly, and sympathetic. Listen to their thoughts, ask questions to discover their needs and interests. Do favors for them. Bite your tongue when you feel it coiling to give them a lashing. Try to make friends with people. Experience what it is like to be a friend.

Strategy 5: Practice Depending on Others Place yourself in a role where you are clearly dependent on another person. Take a committee assignment where you must take instructions. Acknowledge your dependency to others. Examine your feelings while following orders. Seek to be directed, then carry out your assignments. Imagine yourself being completely dependent. Think of yourself only as a subordinate.

Strategy 6: Practice Relating to Nonattackers Identify your own attack squadron, then avoid confining your relationships to those in it. Seek individuals from each of the other five styles and try to get to know them. Seek environmental contacts that force you to be nice, take on visible obligations, follow through on your commitments and reward you for doing so.

How Do You Get the Attacker to Want to Change?

To motivate the attacker to pursue the six strategies for moving closer to the achiever, you should follow the same six key steps to create change discussed in chapter 9 for the Commander. You should:

1. Accept him and thus gain his trust;

2. This will make him feel psychologically safe;

3. When he feels safe, he will begin to conduct research on himself;

4. His research will lead him toward self-understanding;

5. After he understands himself, he can then set goals he desires to reach, to change to; and

6. He should take specific actions to try to change.

To implement these six steps, you must begin in a modified "Attacker Change Style." You should be moderately directive, straightforward, outspoken and tough. When he denies your authority and stings you with his cynicism, you must acknowledge his assaults, brush them off, stand firm, and come back at him with moderate forcefulness. In a sense, you should let him sock you until he exhausts himself, then get down to business. By this method, he will realize that he is not going to hurt or scare you, and more significantly, that you are not going to hurt him. At this point, trust begins. Then you can become more accepting and nondirective. Until you begin to develop trust and equality in your relationship, you must be moderately directive.

SUMMARY

To assist you in mastering your ability to work effectively with attackers, try to recall the major features of this chapter and summarize them in your own words.

1. What are the major dimensions of the attacker's leadership style?

2. Where does he fit best?

3. What are the general consequences of his leadership practices?

4. How can you get along best with attackers?

5. How can attackers change?

6. How can you motivate attackers to want to change?

Look back over the chapter now to check your summary with my analysis of attacker leaders. Think again of attacker leaders you know personally. How accurately does the description given here meet with your observations? Try to get to know more thoroughly the attackers you thought of to improve your understanding of human behavior.

CHAPTER 11

The Avoider's Leadership Style

Disliking responsibility, the avoider is a true nonleader. As a teacher, for instance, he does not stimulate his students. He does not challenge them for fear that, if he awakens his students, they will stir up problems for him. He would rather lecture from detailed notes than allow questions or discussions.

Similarly, as a parent leader, the avoider routinizes his children's lives. He does not lead them toward positive accomplishments. He negatively reacts to his children's fresh efforts, often raising their fears to the point they stop trying to be self-reliant. He discourages their initiative.

As a military leader, the avoider seeks cover behind orders so he can hide. Likewise, the avoider-coach abdicates responsibility, placing the burden of winning or losing on his assistants and players. If they do not fill the leadership void, nothing happens.

Goal Setting

The avoider-leader dislikes setting goals for himself or his subordinates; therefore, he gets others to set them. Thus, if the goals are not attained, the others are held responsible, not him. A second technique he uses to hide from setting objectives is to select jobs where the goals are already set and are easy to accomplish.

Decision Making

The avoider procrastinates in making decisions because he fears he will make poor ones. Accordingly, he does not seek participation from subordinates. He encourages them to go their own way, and to let him do the same.

If the avoider must make a decision, he often clouds the issues by bringing up irrelevant points and finding possible weakness. One rather frustrated president of a large discount chain commented:

> I know well the kind of guy you're talking about. I have one for a brother-in-law working in my New York office. He wants everybody's advice in confusing the issues so nothing will happen! My brother-in-law doesn't want good information to make decisions with, because if he had the facts laid out, everyone could see the alternatives, and he would be on the spot to make a decision. So he positions things so the discussions are ambiguous and the alternatives are equal. Then we can't blame him for failing to make a decision. This also gives him an excuse to get his boss and everyone else involved so that they will run the job for him.

Feedback on Performance

The avoider rarely gives feedback to his subordinates. If he does, it is invisible except to the well-trained eye. In the most casual manner, he engages his subordinates in passing conversation about a topic completely unrelated to the problem without explicitly mentioning the issue at hand, then drops this issue completely. In this manner, he feels he has disposed of his responsibility to evaluate his subordinates' performance. Nevertheless, he talks glibly in such modern management terms as "management-by-objectives" and "performance appraisal." However, when his boss asks him if he would like to use one of these tools in his department, he gives a thousand excuses why it should not be done. If a system of goal-setting is forced upon him, he sets such general objectives that he cannot be pinned down.

Conflict-Resolution

The avoider-leader strenuously shies away from conflicts. If two of his subordinates are in a fight, he says, "Well, that's their problem. It's none of my business. Let them work it out!'' If one of his subordinates comes to him with a complaint, he listens, denies any wrongdoing, then changes the subject or breaks off the conversation.

One avoider, who was the manager of the Plant Safety Department of a small machine manufacturing firm in New York, illustrated these points well. Interestingly, his department was in charge of fire protection, policing, health and safety. He was constantly worried that something was going wrong in his company. One afternoon while he was walking through the plant, a fire broke out in the assembly area. Flames and screams filled the air. The assistant safety manager quickly appeared and directed the activity. The fire was extinguished and calm restored. During the fire, the avoider-leader, the plant safety manager, hid behind a large set of boxes, and did not reappear until things were settled. The conflict was too threatening, so he escaped!

Empacation

The avoider-manager has a distant style of relating to others. He seldom gets to know others because he keeps his relationships on a surface level. He stays detached to avoid being hurt. As a result, his subordinates feel uncomfortable around him. They feel they cannot be themselves, that they have to be careful, for otherwise they would shake him up.

Communications   The avoider-leader seldom expresses his thoughts because if he did, he would incur risk. If he must speak, he talks incessantly and almost incoherently. His ideas are confusing, and his logic seems to disappear as he jumps from one topic to another. He talks and talks but never says anything.

Listening   The avoider ignores his subordinates, for he believes that, if he hears nothing, he risks nothing. When his boss talks about accepted procedures, however, he listens carefully, for he wants to learn how to hide behind the rules.

Supportiveness—Humor   Relatively detached and unresponsive, the avoider is shy and retiring, almost introverted. He shows little warmth or supportiveness toward his subordinates. His humor is passive and inhibited. If he tells a joke, he is likely to forget the punch line. He frequently prefaces his attempts at humor by saying, "Oh, you've probably heard this one before, haven't you? It really isn't much." He also finds it difficult to laugh easily. If something strikes him as funny, he gives a sheepish smile but not a full-fledged belly laugh.

Hostility—Temper He communicates anxiety and a lack of confidence to his subordinates, not by an explosive temper, but by releasing fear through nervous displays of tension. He becomes tense when he is pushed into a corner, but even then, he often deprecates his own talents and withdraws. He does not get visibly mad.

Defensiveness The avoider is a master defense player. He spends a great deal of energy staying out of trouble because of his low capacity to accept humiliation. He selects nebulous situational factors to blame for his mistakes, seldom accepting responsibility for failures.

Sensitivity—Empathy The avoider is disinterested in developing his skills in empathy, because he has no motivation to work closely with others. Thus, he has little sensitivity to nonverbal communications or other subtle forms of personal relationships. Accordingly, he sees little reason to attend seminars on leadership skills. He might say, "As long as you do your job and don't cause anyone problems, what do you need to study personality for? If people would mind their own business, things would go along fine." Open group discussions about feelings and emotions, such as encounter or T-groups, terrify avoiders. Nevertheless, they often are sympathetic to those in trouble for they know well how it feels to be in pain. They are more sympathetic than empathetic.

Where Do Avoiders Fit?

Best-Fit Situations When the environmental stimuli which confront the avoider are predictable and stable, he is able to hide from risks and responsibilities. When the organizational structure is so well defined that the avoider can understand his duties exactly and take little responsibility, he is extremely productive. Consequently, the avoider excels in jobs that are repetitive, for he is safe while working on low-risk assignments. He performs well as a clerical employee, key-punch operator, typist, production worker, or bookkeeper. His personal needs are satisfied by the organization to the degree it regulates his life—the more regulation, the more he is fulfilled and effective.

Worst-Fit Situations   The avoider-leader is a misfit in a performer organizational setting. When the situation demands conspicuous displays, flashy actions, and shrewd maneuvers, the avoider falls flat on his face. Because he craves to be a shadow, rapid public exposure accompanied by aggressive demands for initiative panic the avoider and he performs poorly.

Best-Matched People   The avoider-leader gets along best with the commander. The commander directs his life, takes the risks out of his work, and does not expect close or creative relations. They both prefer the orderly to the confusing, the detailed to the abstract, the safe to the risky. These complementary needs cement their mutual satisfaction.

Worst-Matched People   The avoider gets along least well with the performer. The performer craves attention, recognition, risks, and visibility. These activities threaten the essence of the avoider's life because he has difficulty hiding from the performer's efforts to pull him into the spotlight. In a marriage, for example, the avoider spouse prefers to stay home and watch TV, while the performer wants to socialize. One of my avoider patients, for example, was married to a performer wife. During the first two years of their marriage, as he described it,

> Our relationship was painfully strained. She always wanted to do things, to go places; I preferred to stay home with our new baby. She was always the life of the party, while I usually sat by myself. Finally, we figured out if she worked, she'd get out of the home and escape her misery in sitting around the house all day. This worked

well for six months, but then she fell in love with her boss and had an affair with him. I caught them! We're separated now and trying to work it out.

This example indicates the contrary needs of avoiders and performers.

General Consequences of the Avoider's Style of Leadership

In mixed situations, the avoider produces the following general results.

Efficiency Doing a job in an orderly and precise manner is the avoider's strong suit. He is efficient. Organizational procedures are followed exactly for he mimics his boss's directives with the skill of a well-tuned robot. He is so efficient, in fact, that he often is ineffective because he comes bogged down in meaningless details.

Morale Generally his subordinates have low morale. His subordinates disrespect him rather than hate him. The avoider does not involve his subordinates in the work of the organization. They are not encouraged to grow or to test their talents. Consequently, they find little excitement in their work.

Personal Growth The avoider does not create management talent. Although he does not actively suppress those under him from doing what they wish, he does not encourage them to grow, learn, become more skilled and experienced. He discourages his subordinates' efforts at self-renewal by highlighting failures they might encounter and by expressing doubts about their abilities. His pessimism clouds their thinking.

Organizational Growth Environmental changes threaten the avoider, so he does not adapt to situational demands, but rather ignores them. His organization, then, loses touch with the outside world. Left under his direction, his department will slowly become invisible.

At one of my seminars, I met an avoider whose reluctance to

respond to changing needs almost cost her organization several hundred thousand dollars. Rose was the well-liked, very efficient manager of a bank's key-punch operation. A nervous middle-aged single woman of somewhat corpulent girth, Rose was as shy as she was efficient. She had an idea for organizational change that would save installation of a second large computer the bank wanted to purchase. But she expressed her plan in the seminar only after much encouragement from me. I urged her to mention it to her boss the next day. A week later, I asked Rose what had happened. She sheepishly answered, "Nothing." She had not told her boss the idea. After several similar occurrences, I finally said to her boss, "Rose has a wonderful idea I think you should ask her about." He did, and her idea ended up saving the bank $14,000 a month. Over a six-year period, that amounts to more than one-million dollars! Her passivity almost kept the company from growing by a rather large amount.

Overall Effectiveness   For most situations, the avoider-leader provides poor results. Most managers, in fact, select the avoider as the worst subordinate they have ever had. The avoider—as coach, parent, teacher, or administrator—takes a disproportionate share of his boss's time, for the boss needs to decide almost everything the avoider does, then to follow up to make sure that he does it.

How Do You Best Get Along With the Avoider-Leader?

As his Subordinate   The avoider-leader prefers his subordinates to be avoiders so they will follow his goals in a safe, inconspicuous manner. The avoider mother, for example, prefers her children to be avoiders, for they present her with relatively few problems. The avoider-teacher likes her students to be passive, quiet, and orderly, for then she can shrink behind her passive lectures and formalized class procedures. The avoider-military leader wants his followers to be disciplined by the military rules, not by his direction. The avoider-coach rewards his assistant coaches and players who do their jobs unquestioningly. If you want to be well liked by your avoider-boss, behave as an avoider would. Nonavoiders in the organization will not respect you, but he will.

As his Superior The best boss for an avoider is the commander. The avoider wants to be led, to be given detailed activities for which the means to the goals are as clearly stated as the goals themselves. This control is provided by the commander. To manage the avoider successfully, you must become directive and systematic. You should not engage him in discussion, but nicely tell him what to do.

As his Peer To relate effectively as the avoider's peer, you should behave much as his preferred subordinate—meek and passive. By not infringing on his territory, you please him most.

How Can the Avoider Change?

If you are an avoider leader and want to change to become more of an achiever, my experience in changing avoiders suggests seven key strategies you can follow.[1]

Strategy 1: Practice Acting as If You Were Self-Confident Make a thorough list of all of your good points. Stretch your imagination, develop as long a list as you can. Emphasize your positive qualities because this will help to change your self-image.

At the beginning of each day, think of something you would really like to do, but might avoid out of fear. Take five minutes to imagine yourself doing the job extremely well. See yourself as relaxed, confident, skilled, and positive while performing the tasks. See yourself enjoying completing the projects successfully.

Practice acting as if your ideas were valuable by speaking up in groups, stating your opinions openly, trusting your own thoughts and desires. Act as if you were confident of your skills.

Be sure to examine how you feel during each of your attempts to change. Be sure to congratulate yourself after each of your successes. Remember, a small step is a big success.

Strategy 2: Practice Taking Risks When you find yourself seeking safety, take a moderate risk. Accept an assignment where you have a moderate risk of failing and which is not completely defined by

---

1. If you are an avoider and want to enhance these tendencies then seek out an avoider environment.

rules and procedures. Try things you have avoided most of your life. For example, if you have not learned how to drive, do so; or if you have had bad grammar and poor speaking abilities, seek training. List those things you have worried about most of your life, then begin to do something about them, remembering it takes time to change.

When you are afraid, think about the worst possible outcome if you take a risk and fail. For example, if you hide from public speaking, what could happen if you signed up for a speaking course? People might laugh at you; perhaps you would look stupid; or your wife would be ashamed of you. What is the likelihood of these negative events occurring? How badly would they hurt you? Take some risks.

Strategy 3: Practice Doing It Now   When faced with a decision, do not procrastinate. Do it now. Make a big sign that says, "DO IT NOW!" Place it where you can see it constantly. List the decisions you must face, think them through as best you can and choose between alternatives. When you start to delay, say to yourself, "Don't avoid self-responsibility: do it now."

Strategy 4: Practice Being Independent and Domineering   Select several situations during each day when you can practice being independent from others' control. Say what you think; run your own life; direct your own behavior. Go even further by actually trying to dominate others. See if you can tell others what to do. Then, ask yourself how you felt while doing it.

Strategy 5: Practice Seeking Honest Feedback   Actively expose yourself to feedback. Listen without blocking out what you do not want to hear. Ask several friends if they would help you in your attempts to become more effective by telling you what they think are your major strengths and weaknesses. Make an appointment with your boss to ask him the same questions. Ask your spouse to risk giving you some honest evaluations. Try to write down what you hear. Study your notes. Ask yourself how you feel about the process of seeking feedback and about the content you hear.

Strategy 6: Practice Facing Conflicts Decide who your major conflicts are with, then go to at least two of those involved and say, "I want to try to solve our conflicts. I would like to try to understand what has caused them and what we can do to cure them. I know there are two sides to every story, and my goal is to try to improve myself and our relationship. What do you think about our problems?" Just reading this suggestion probably scares you to death. Think carefully about what might happen if you faced a few conflicts. How bad would it be? Think how good it will feel if you succeed. Do it now!

Strategy 7: Practice Getting Into Achievement Situations Try to find individuals you think are achievers, then make an effort to associate with them. Study them, copy them, learn from them. Seek environments that are changing, complex, and unpredictable. Experiment with activities that have few rules, require discretion, and make you nervous. Then examine how you feel in these situations.

Do not worry about overdoing your change efforts, because your natural self-protective devices will prevent you from following these seven strategies for changing the avoider as extensively as they are stated here. In fact, you must push yourself firmly just to make small steps in these directions, so try them. You will be surprised how easy it is after you get started. If you are an avoider and have just read these pages, you should be congratulated, because most avoiders would not take the risks you have just taken by reading these ideas. You have taken risk and self-responsibility.

How Do You Get the Avoider to Want to Change?

To make the avoider want to change, you should follow the same six key steps to create change discussed in chapter 9 (p. 140). You should:
1. Create trust with him by accepting him;
2. Make him feel psychologically safe;
3. Stimulate him to conduct research on himself;
4. Help him understand his own personality;
5. Encourage him to set goals; and
6. Motivate the avoider to try to change.
The unique method of implementing these steps with the avoider

should begin with a softened commander style of leadership. You should be clear, directive, certain, structured, and highly supportive. As you guide the avoider along the seven strategies for becoming more like an achiever, you can switch to a more nonstructured, achiever approach. As he takes initiative to direct his own life, you can withdraw your control. This transition should be gradual.

Your initial efforts to motivate him to take self-assertive actions must not be punitive, for this would create too much anxiety and, thus, resistance on his part. You must positively reinforce him by emphasizing his strengths.

Similarly, your initial efforts to motivate the avoider to want to change will not succeed if you are too passive. If you act as an avoider with him, you simply reward his past behavior, you do not encourage change.

To get the avoider to take action, then, you must at first gradually instigate activities for him; hold his hand; support him; encourage him; and teach him to stand on his own two feet. He needs support and direction from you until he can provide it for himself.

SUMMARY

To help you in mastering your ability to work effectively with the avoider, try to recall the major features of this chapter and summarize them in your own words.

1. What are the key aspects of the avoider's leadership style?

2. In which situations does he fit best?

3. What are the general consequences of his leadership practices?

4. How do you best get along with the avoider?

5. How can the avoider change?

6. How can you motivate the avoider to want to change?

Look back over this chapter now to check how accurately you understand the avoider-leader. Now try to apply some of these suggestions in your relationships.

CHAPTER 12

The Pleaser's Leadership Style

Goal Setting

The pleaser-leader sets goals that are easy to attain, because he does not want to push his subordinates. Rather, he sets goals that please his subordinates. Realizing that he and his subordinates must produce an acceptable quota to be popular within his company, he attempts to make people happy by producing at least a minimum amount.

Decision Making

The pleaser-leader encourages extensive group participation from his subordinates in making decisions. He wants to know if anyone is upset so he will ask, "Is this worded properly? Does everyone support it?" He establishes many committees which often are used to generate friendships, alleviate tensions, and clarify members' feelings, rather than produce results. He steers discussions away from work so conflicts will not arise. This process takes much time, much talk, and often decisions remain unmade. When he does make a decision, he frequently comes up with solutions that are convenient rather than productive.

Feedback on Performance

The pleaser-leader has an unusual style of giving feedback. He is moderately honest with his subordinates in dealing with his positive feelings, yet he looks the other way when a subordinate makes a mistake.

One executive, a buyer for a large retail firm, commented:

"You know, my boss is a real pleaser-leader. I'll be stuck with a problem and walk down to his office to talk it over with him. He'll pat me on the back, tell me I'm the salt of the earth, that I'm just doing a great job. I leave his office with my chest out, but as I walk down the hall, I ask myself, 'Now what did I go in there for? I feel good, but I didn't solve my problem.' "

Conflict Resolution

The pleaser-leader smooths over conflicts, laughs them off, jokes about them, or pretends they do not exist. These efforts inhibit his subordinates, because they sense that discussing conflicts will somehow hurt the pleaser; thus, they are inclined to say the things that make him feel good.

Empacation

The pleaser-leader is easy to get along with, popular, and well-liked. Unkind words seldom escape from his mouth, for he adjusts his own behavior quickly to accommodate a subordinate's wishes.

There is a fine line, of course, between being truly accepting and having no convictions. In the pleaser's case, this causes many who know him well to feel that he is pleasant but somewhat sneaky and boring. One subordinate said: "After you get to know him, you find out there really isn't much there. He's a mushy marshmallow, soft and sweet with little core to get your teeth into. But, he's easy to be around. He is one of the nicest people I know."

Communications   The pleaser spends a great deal of time talking with others—at coffee, in committee meetings, or simply working on team projects. By the sheer amount of time he spends communicating, he transmits a lot of information. What he says, however, is often unimportant. Because he wants so much to be accepted, he covers his true beliefs in favor of communicating what the listeners want to hear.

Listening The pleaser listens politely to his subordinates. He devotes hours to sympathetically hearing their ideas, positions, and comments. His subordinates, however, often feel that his sympathy is over-flattering, for they know they are not as good as the pleaser tries to make them sound.

Supportiveness—Humor Subordinates feel that their pleaser-manager supports them with his humor. He is seldom aggressive in his jokes, and rather than laughing at them or enjoying their mishaps, he teases only in positive ways. On happy occasions, his humor can be infectious.

Hostility—Temper The pleaser-leader seldom gets angry or makes others mad. Subordinates may disagree, become aggressive or overtly ridicule the pleaser-leader without receiving retaliation. He glosses over hostile remarks, changes the subject, or focuses the aggression on other members of the group.

Defensiveness The pleaser is only slightly defensive. Because he is other-directed, when he is criticized, he usually agrees with the criticism since his convictions are not as important to him as being liked. Since he wants to keep things running smoothly, he seldom protests exposure of his own weaknesses.

Sensitivity—Empathy The pleaser-leader is highly sensitive to the feelings of his subordinates and colleagues. He has a finely-tuned radar system which signals him when he can help someone and, thus, gain friendship.

Where Do Pleasers Fit?

Best-Fit Situations The pleaser can best fulfill his acceptance needs within a loose organizational structure—a pleaser situation—because that gives him the time and freedom to float from one work station to another, performing kind acts which build acceptance for him. The less the pleaser's job environment requires him to be isolated from people, or work alone with ideas or machines, the more effective he is. When his tasks do not constrain him by their noise, pace, or need for concentration, he is able to build friendships. He does only moderately well, then, on predictable, mass-technology jobs, for instance as an assembly-line worker, because they minimize his social contacts. Service, secretarial, and sales jobs that require order filling are examples of situations in which the pleaser fits well.

Worst-Fit Situations   The pleaser is a misfit in attacker environments. Situations which require independence, initiative, disruptions, friction, aggression, competition, and counterproductive efforts seriously violate the pleaser's leadership style. Conflicts paralyze the pleaser and make him ineffective. Tough sales jobs and top leadership positions which require much criticism and action are examples of situations in which the pleaser is miscast.

Best-Matched People   The pleaser is most compatible with other pleasers. They fulfill each other's needs, for by their reciprocal kindness, they build mutual acceptance and satisfaction. They encourage generosity and warmth, agree on easy goals, smooth over their conflicts and give only positive feedback. Thus, they work well together.

Worst-Matched People   The pleaser gets along the most poorly with the attacker. Because an attacker ridicules the pleaser constantly, he blocks the pleaser's major needs. If a pleaser marries an attacker, for instance, they have serious problems because of their great incompatibilities. The pleaser craves warmth, the attacker frigidity. The pleaser wants acceptance, the attacker rejection. The pleaser desires closeness, the attacker distance.

General Consequences of the Pleaser's Style of Leadership

In mixed situations, pleasers produce the following consequences.

Efficiency Generally, the pleaser has little concern for efficiency. If he stresses detailed organization, he might step on his subordinates' toes. Consequently, he encourages informality. His work is often colorful, messy, and informal, never systematic. If his boss forces order upon him, of course, he will become efficient quickly.

Morale The pleaser-leader produces a curious mixture of positive and negative feelings among his subordinates. On the one hand, he establishes an easy-going, friendly work atmosphere which reduces tensions, builds cohesiveness, and establishes informal associations off the job. On the other hand, many of his subordinates do not respect the pleaser, even though they like him personally. They feel he lacks the direction, purpose, and courage needed to set a course for them to follow, and that he is overly nice and unrealistically optimistic. These conflicting forces create moderate morale.

Personal Growth Personal development is not on the pleaser's list of priorities. He is not interested in successful results, so sees little need to try to improve. As long as things are going smoothly, he does not want to rock the boat. Thus, if he can learn of ways to maintain his goal, he will seek new learning experiences. Otherwise, he discourages self-renewal efforts by his subordinates.

Organizational Growth Typically, the pleaser encourages his organization to adapt selectively to its environment by scanning the situations it encounters for forces which might dampen the personal relationships of his staff. Then he adapts well to these stimuli.

Overall Effectiveness The pleaser's organization generally produces below-average results. He runs the department within an organization that creates neither superlative nor horrible outputs. His department is noted for the pleasant relationships of its members, its lack of conflicts, and its somewhat below-average productivity.

How Do You Get Along With the Pleaser-Leader?

As his Subordinate If you want to be approved of by a pleaser-leader, you should behave as a pleaser-subordinate. Agree, cooperate, smooth over problems, do not rock the boat, praise others, and you will do well under the pleaser's direction.

As his Superior To manage the pleaser effectively, you should be nice, yet moderately directive. You must urge him on by reinforcing his popularity and acceptance. You must follow up on your assignments to him to ensure that he does not drop them in favor of smoothing over disturbed friendships. If you reward the pleaser constantly, he will strive to fulfill your wishes, and he will be moderately productive.

As his Peer To get along well with the pleaser as his peer, you should behave just like his subordinates—as a pleaser. If you are kind, considerate, and friendly, you will get along together.

How Can the Pleaser Change?

If you are a pleaser-leader and want to become more of an achiever, there are six key strategies you can follow to assist in your efforts to change.[1]

Strategy 1: Practice Being a Deviant To fight your craving to be accepted, concentrate on several situations in which you can try to be different, to be an outcast. Say to yourself, ''I do not want to be accepted by this group. What can I do to be rejected?'' Do not worry about being especially obnoxious, for you will barely ruffle their feathers since this type of behavior is so foreign to you.

Strategy 2: Practice Being Self-Directed When you notice yourself automatically following another's lead, stop yourself and say,

---

1. If you are a pleaser and want to enhance these needs, then, of course seek your best-fit-adjustment situation—a pleaser environment.

"This is a chance to direct my own life. What do I want to do?" Try to follow your own desires. Ignore others' opinions. To overcome your tendencies to be a yes-man, to be wishy-washy, to be unable to say no, stand up for yourself. Turn down requests in which you are uninterested. Practice saying no.

Strategy 3: Practice Developing Convictions Decide what the major issues are that you deal with in your life—at work, with your spouse, children, friends and hobbies—then formulate your own beliefs about each of them. Think them through. Examine them carefully, then develop your own philosophy about each of these issues. By developing your own convictions, you will not be so easily persuaded by others.

Strategy 4: Practice Acting Mean To be more honest in your relations with others, try being mean. Purposely say hostile things. Select several occasions in which you can most easily kick sand in someone's face. Give and seek negative feedback from others. When one of your subordinates or friends makes a mistake, do not shy from it. Point it out to him. Discuss it fully. Tell him you are disappointed. Again, do not worry about losing all your friends, because for you to act tough enough to cause serious problems will be very difficult.

Strategy 5: Practice Confronting Conflicts When you have a disagreement, do not smooth it over or laugh it off. Go directly to the person you are having the conflict with and confront him— but with love. Tell him you would like to face the problem and see if you can work it out to improve your relationship. Admit that you are angry and upset. Admit to yourself that the other person is also probably mad. Select several disagreements you are now having and make a concerted effort to face them constructively.

Strategy 6: Practice Setting High Goals To overcome your timidity, think of several areas of your life in which you can set moderately high goals. Take some risks by exerting yourself. Make a commitment openly to try to reach a challenging objective. Do not pretend you did not want something when you worked hard for it and failed. Expose yourself to nonpleaser situations. Take an assignment that prevents you from working closely with other people. Seek a task which forces you to take the responsibility for its completion, rather than depend on others to direct you.

How Do You Get the Pleaser to Want to Change?

To motivate the pleaser to want to change to gain more achiever qualities you should follow the same six key steps to create change discussed in chapter 9 (p. 135). You should:
 1. Create trust with him by accepting him;
 2. Make him feel psychologically safe;
 3. Stimulate him to conduct research on himself;
 4. Help him understand his own personality;
 5. Encourage him to set goals; and
 6. Motivate the pleaser to take steps to change.

To implement these steps most effectively, given the unique features of the pleaser's style, you should be moderately directive and extremely nice. You need to push the pleaser into action, to substitute your strength for his weakness, for he does not naturally desire to improve. While doing so, you must be warm, friendly, and considerate. Your patience will be tested, for you must devote considerable time listening to the pleaser, building his ego, and praising him for his steps toward self-renewal. As he becomes more independent, you can become more nondirective—more like the achiever-leader.

SUMMARY

How well can you recall the major features of the pleaser-leader? Test your understanding of the pleaser by writing down your own summary of this chapter. After completing your review, go back and skim the major topic headings to measure your results.

1. What are the major aspects of the pleaser's leadership style?

2. In which situations does he fit best?

3. What are the general consequences of his leadership practices?

4. How do you best get along with the pleaser?

5. How can the pleaser change?

6. How can you cause the pleaser to want to change?

CHAPTER 13

The Performer's Leadership Style

Goal Setting

The performer is not recognized for either breaking old records or reaching new lows. He scouts out the proper rules of behavior and other management practices, then makes sure his subordinates follow them. To set his objectives, he studies carefully what his superiors expect, then he formulates acceptable plans for his department. His goals normally involve the attainment of prestige and are moderately challenging.

Decision Making

The performer-leader makes his own decisions, but gets his subordinates to feel they have participated by using psuedoparticipation. After he formulates his plans, he calls in his subordinates and casually brings up the decision without directly asking for their opinions. He, nevertheless, gauges their reactions, for he knows that by talking about a decision with them, they will feel like part of the team. He might include some of their ideas, however, if they are tangential to the main thrust of his decision.

Feedback on Performance

The performer specializes in giving confusing and somewhat dishonest feedback to his subordinates. As one subordinate commented, "You can be talking with that fox about a subject, and suddenly you begin to feel a little uneasy. You are not sure if he is joking or serious when he makes a comment about your work. You feel uneasy, but you're not sure why." He seldom expresses his evaluations candidly because he prefers to remain uncommitted.

Conflict Resolution

The performer leader seeks compromises to resolve conflicts. Accordingly, he changes his ideas, feigns agreement, partially modifies his behavior to suit potentially troublesome situations, and tries to sell his subordinates on his ideas. He does not bring problems out into the open. He prefers safe compromises.

Empacation

Interestingly, those who do not know him well think highly of the performer. However, one subordinate put it, "The more you get to know him, the more you realize that much of what he does is to manage his image. He is not sincere. He lacks integrity."

Communications The performer-leader formulates his objectives clearly, then designs his communications so that he gets his message across without being obvious. He distorts his messages to accomplish the results he desires.

Listening The performer's skill as a listener comes from his desire to calculate a response, to maneuver the conversation and to change the point of view of the speaker. He hears enough to figure out a clever image-building comment, or to make himself come out ahead in the conversation. He does not listen, however, to understand, to see his subordinates' point of view, or to learn about his subordinates' assumptions and reasoning. He listens to get ahead.

Supportiveness—Humor The performer has a sly and witty sense of humor; it is not genuinely warm or supportive. Instead, he uses his humor as a tool to evoke popularity, to drive home a point, or to change the subject so that it will not focus upon his weaknesses. In addition, he can make negative, attacking comments that are so well camouflaged they seem funny, and thereby, not lose respect for talking behind others' backs.

Hostility—Temper   To maintain his image, the performer seldom loses his temper. When he does, he becomes tight and stiff rather than vocal. If he becomes annoyed in a meeting, for example, his face may redden or he may draw firmly on his notepad without saying a word.

Defensiveness   The performer-manager is moderately defensive, for he seldom talks about his weaknesses. If attacked, he listens for a short while, then tries to change the subject, hints that it was someone else's responsibility, or uses moderate force to close down the criticism.

Sensitivity   The performer-leader is quite good at perceiving the feelings of his subordinates, because he understands this will (1) get him results, (2) endear his subordinates to him, (3) provide him with more information about them and (4) enable him to manipulate and control them more easily.

Where Do Performers Fit?

Best-Fit Situations   The performer functions most effectively when his work environment is moderately stable and connects him with prestigious people, positions, and things. The more visible his role, the better he does. The performer excels on jobs which encourage him to look good, speak well, analyze group norms, be a clever conversationalist, and to have connections with important people. Political, social, sales, administrative, civic, and public relations types of environmental contacts satisfy the performer's needs to impress and maneuver. Consequently, he does well in these situations.

Worst-Fit Situations   When the performer is placed in an avoider situation, he functions poorly. If he is urged to hide, to select routine, easy assignments, and to not make deals, he is severely frustrated. Repetitive tasks drive him crazy for he has little chance to prove himself. He can do little to shine when rules, organizational structures, or technologies restrict his maneuvering. His frantic striving is smothered in these situations for his freedom to win prestige is restricted.

Best-Matched People Mutual aid is provided by one performer for another, because they build their images and arrange their environments in such a way that they help each other accomplish their goals. Their common styles blend well; they both like prestige, striving, wise use of their time, and image management. Two performers as husband-wife, student-teacher, coach-player, parent-child, or boss-subordinate form a best-fit adjustment relationship because they reward each other for acting out their needs.

Worst-Matched People The performer has the poorest relations with the avoider, because the avoider provides little recognition, respect or opportunity for the performer to display his wares. The avoider's sterile public exposure offers nothing to the performer in his efforts to climb upward. In fact, the avoider places an anchor on the performer's striving for prestige.

General Consequences of the Performer's Leadership Style In a mixture of types of people and situations, the performer leader produces the following general results.

Efficiency The performer functions with moderate efficiency. He is as orderly as he needs to be to please those in positions of power. As long as it promotes his upward climb, he will be systematic, even though he does not have his heart in it. His natural inclination is to be somewhat messy and unclear in his work patterns.

Morale Subordinates of the performer have mixed emotions about working for him. They enjoy the prestige he brings to their department and the glamour of the work he guides them toward. Yet, he does not produce positive enjoyment among his staff, for he creates a lack of trust and integrity with his subordinates. They react quite negatively to his hypocrisy. These two forces combine to produce only medium morale.

Personal Growth   The performer encourages his subordinates to develop their skills so they can contribute to the results which will make him look good. They are allowed moderate participation and opportunities for experiencing self-reliance. Consequently, the performer fosters only modest personal growth in his subordinates. Their growth is directed, of course, toward becoming performers themselves.

Organizational Growth   The performer takes some risks to keep in tune with his environmental constraints so he will be able to get ahead. He seldom takes bold steps but rarely waits too long before responding to environmental changes. His organization adapts modestly well to situational events. He is especially skillful at working with the political, public relations, and image-making segments of his environment, for these are the keys to his own success.

Overall Effectiveness   The performer gains above-average results in his work. His strenuous efforts to acquire success so others will praise him causes him to work day and night to perform well. By his keen energy, sensitivity to political maneuvers, shrewd deal-making, and skillful image management, he manipulates his way to high levels of success. His overall results are dampened, however, by his Machiavellian gestures which destroy the intrinsic motivation and loyalty of his subordinates. Following his lead, they soon begin to look out for themselves and to promote their own advancement over the organization's goals. This modest commitment of his subordinates detracts from the performer's zealous charge toward successful results.

How Do You Best Get Along With the Performer-Leader?

As his Superior   To manage the performer effectively, without trying to change him, you should give him visible assignments, praise him publicly and frequently, show him how he will move upward, make special, secretive deals with him, and engage him in joint image management. These rewards stimulate his desires to strive for productivity.

At the same time, you should make sure that he completes the tasks he begins, that his personal goals do not take precedence over the organization's goals, and that he is not hurting you behind your back. By firmly controlling these possibilities, you ensure that he will stay on a productive course.

As his Subordinate You should behave very much like a performer to get along well as his subordinate. The more you maneuver with him, always letting him look good, the more he will reward your efforts.

As his Peer Again, performer behavior wins the performer's heart. Talk with him about ways of getting ahead. Illustrate your accomplishments, connections, and other assets, so he can see what you can do for him. Offer him hints he can use to get ahead. He will value you highly for this.

How Can the Performer Change?

My experience suggests that, if you are a performer-leader and want to change to become more of an achiever, there are five key strategies you should follow.

Strategy 1: Practice Slowing Down Fight your urge to get everything done immediately. Evaluate carefully how important it is to finish the tasks you are working on. Try to rank your projects in priorities, then fit them to a time schedule. When you have done this, drop the last 25 percent of your list of tasks. This will give you a cushion in your time plan.

Concentrate on doing one thing at a time. When you are talking with someone, do not read a memo, make a phone call, or try to do two things simultaneously. Do one thing at a time, and do it well. Take thirty minutes each day to do something for the pure joy of doing it, not for the payoff it gives you. Go for walks, listen to music, look at birds, or read poetry, for example.

Strategy 2: Practice Being Honest Practice telling people what you really think. When someone asks you to commit yourself to a position and you find yourself beginning to evade a direct answer, try to substitute the truth for a lie.

Try not to give false flattery, laugh when you do not think it is funny, to "brown-nose" your boss, or to act overly nice to someone you strongly dislike. Practice taking a stand and revealing your true beliefs instead of those most accepted.

Strategy 3: Practice Not Showing Off When you notice yourself bragging about your talents, boasting of your successes, dropping names, illustrating your skills to make an impression, ask yourself why you are doing this. Say to yourself, "Will they like me just as much if I do not try to exaggerate my image?" Select two events during each day on which to practice being direct and honest, rather than flashy, polished, and self-advertising. Try not to buy the latest clothes. Try to wear things that are out of fashion. Purposely, ignore the latest gossip, so you will not be able to one-up your associates.

Strategy 4: Practice Not Manipulating Others Try to take credit only for your own successes, not others. Similarly, accept the blame for your failures instead of pushing them onto others. When a tough job has to be done, do not trick someone else into doing it for you. Take the responsibility yourself. When you catch yourself manipulating another, try instead to tell him honestly what you would like him to do and why you desire his commitment. It is also helpful if you review major events of each day to determine the extent you were honest versus calculating. Then plan how you can be more genuine the next day.

Strategy 5: Practice Doing Those Things You Believe In When evaluating your goals or selecting your next assignments to work on, make two lists. One list should contain those projects you deeply believe in, that you really feel are worthwhile and that you intrinsically would love to do. The other list should contain those tasks that will bring you the most prestige, recognition, public exposure, and return on your investment of time and effort. Now throw away your "Prestige List," and work for several months only on those projects you intrinsically believe in and not those that give you external or extrinsic rewards. To assist in developing your genuine-interest list, ask yourself: "What is really important to do?" "How helpful to others will the results be?" "Is this what I really enjoy doing, no matter what the rewards?" Try to be problem-centered versus self-centered.

How Do You Get the Performer to Want to Change?

If you have a performer you want to change into more of an achiever, you should follow the same six key steps to create change discussed in chapter 9 (p. 140). You should:
1. Create trust with him by accepting him;
2. Make him feel psychologically safe;
3. Stimulate him to conduct research on himself;
4. Help him understand his own personality;
5. Encourage him to set goals; and
6. Motivate the performer to try to change.

To implement these steps effectively, begin your coaching efforts by being sensitive to the performer's image, manners, reputation and need to impress. According to his particular needs, build him up, reward him constantly, let him save face graciously when you indicate you see some weaknesses in him, act respectfully toward him, be proper and mannerly, and show him that, by becoming more of an achiever, he will gain greater results and prestige in the long-run, without having to strive for it.

When the performer becomes noticeably evasive, back off and try again when he is more settled.

Play his game of being flattering, and thus dishonest, as long as you have to; however, move toward honesty and candor as soon as you can. As you create trust with the performer, he will become more honest with you. As he realizes you value authenticity and integrity, he will act more this way than usual just to gain your approval. Reward him for his efforts.

His self-awareness will only come gradually, so do not try to push him faster than his self-esteem can carry him. It is critical for the performer to feel highly respected. To discover he is not is shattering. Thus, he should be allowed to discover his true self at his own speed.

SUMMARY

Test your understanding of the performer-leader by trying to write down the major features of this chapter below.

1. What are the key aspects of the performer's leadership style?

2. In which situations does he fit best?

3. What are the general consequences of his leadership practices?

4. How do you best get along with the performer?

5. How can the performer change?

6. How can you motivate the performer to want to change?

Look back over this chapter now to check how accurately you understand the performer-leader. Which chapter was easiest for you to summarize so far? Why was one easier for you to recall than the others? Generally, you can remember most easily the chapter that describes you best.

CHAPTER 14

The Achiever's Leadership Style

Goal Setting

The achiever-leader sets high, yet realistic goals for himself and his subordinates. In setting a goal, he asks: (1) Is the goal worthwhile, (2) attainable, (3) challenging, and (4) realistic? He establishes his goals thoughtfully.

Decision Making

The achiever-leader makes decisions with the relevant participation of those of his subordinates who have something important to contribute or who will be significantly affected by the decision. He asks for questions and ideas in such a way that his subordinates know he is seriously interested in their opinions. Consequently, they are not fearful of offering suggestions. Because of his honest approach, subordinates feel trusted and willing to take part, to put themselves into the decision and encouraged to gather additional facts regarding the possible outcomes of the decision.

Feedback on Performance

Because of his desire for challenge, his self-confidence, and his commitment to his goals, the achiever-leader examines his own and his subordinates' accomplishments carefully. He seeks and gives a lot of feedback. He asks, "How are we doing?" "What is our progress?" "What are the problems we have?" To respond to these questions, subordinates must think through the answers, provide explanations for the results, and see how their superior reacts to their performance. The achiever-leader, therefore, motivates his subordinates to be concerned about openness, accountability, performance, and evaluation.

Because of their constant checking and rechecking of the accuracy and meaning of the information regarding their performance, the feedback between an achiever and his subordinates is continuous, follows quickly after actions are taken, and is well understood by both parties (John W. Atkinson and Normal T. Feather, *A Theory of Achievement Motivation*, 1966).

Conflict Resolution

When his subordinates have disagreements, the achiever leader usually confronts the conflicts directly. He attempts to understand what happened, without judging or controlling those involved. Instead of "blocking out" comments or trying to distort the other person's views, he listens openly. Since he is self-confident, he tries to *understand* why the problems occurred, to evaluate the *consequences*, and to determine the best *solutions*. He attempts to *discover*, "How can we solve these dilemmas?" "What can we do to make our relationship more effective?"

When a subordinate becomes angry at an achiever-boss, he says to himself, "The last time I messed up, my boss came right down and talked about it. He tried to help solve the problem, and it worked out pretty well. I'll go by his office and see if I can tell him I am upset with him." As this process of honest exchanging takes place, the achiever-leader and his subordinates begin to feel relaxed, spontaneous, and trusting toward one another. Thus, they are able to resolve their conflicts easily.

Empacation

Communications   The achiever-leader explores his feelings and communicates them accurately to his subordinates, he relates to others with candor. Believing that in the long run people feel most at ease when you are honest with them, he attempts to (1) do what he says he will do; (2) explain the things he is doing; and (3) discuss why he is doing it. His communication, therefore, is an accurate reflection of what is going on inside of him. His nonverbal communication—his gestures—are accurate portrayals of his inner beliefs.

Listening The achiever listens openly without tuning out the other person. He makes his point and then tries to understand what the other person is saying. He asks questions such as, ''Would you help me understand what you mean by that?'' ''Why do you disagree?'' ''Would you explain that a little more for me?''

Interestingly, when a subordinate is listened to, he generally feels he is being given a chance to have his day in court, and he, in turn, starts to listen.

Supportiveness—Humor The achiever-leader relates with others in a warm and supportive manner. By his humor he reveals to others that he accepts them for what they are and has confidence in them.

I was invited by an older officer of a large computer firm to talk to the president and the board of directors. During lunch, before the speech, the officer, in a very confident manner, described his boss, the other members of the board, their experiences, and interests. By his supportive behavior, he implied that he was happy I was going to speak. His achiever style made me genuinely feel that I would do a good job, and that they would like what I would say and I performed better than usual.

In another situation, however, the vice-president of marketing for a large retail firm, who was an avoider, asked me to speak to his fellow officers. As we discussed the meeting, his mouth shook, he repeatedly asked if I needed anything and if I thought they would understand what I was going to say. His negative, fearful approach made me nervous, lowered my confidence, decreased my enthusiasm and my results.

Hostility—Temper Being mild-tempered, the achiever is not overly aggressive toward others. When he becomes angry, he approaches the person with whom he is angry, and says something like, ''John,

I feel upset about what happened. Maybe I didn't understand all of the dimensions of the case. Can you help me understand why this happened?'' By confronting a crisis when it occurs, he catches most of his problems when they are small, and he relieves his anxieties as they occur. Thus, he has only a small reservoir of hostilities which can flow forth and build into a volatile temper.

Defensiveness   The achiever is relatively open-minded, listens to ideas that oppose his own, admits his weaknesses and is nondefensive as compared to others.

Sensitivity   Since the achiever receives much feedback and explores himself carefully, he develops the skill to accurately perceive others' feelings.

Where Do the Achievers Fit?

Best-Fit Situations   The achiever-leader operates most successfully when the events he encounters are complex, varied, unpredictable, and realistic. He enjoys the challenge of uncertainty for it makes him exert maximum effort to reach his goals. If his environment is stable, he loses interest in his work and performs poorly.

Similarly, if the organization is structured so formally that it eliminates variety and spontaneous action by the achiever, he performs poorly, for he needs to be able to insert his own personality into his work; therefore, he operates most successfully when he is given a high degree of discretion in performing his job.

Worst-Fit Situations   The achiever fits worst in a commander environment. When things are clearly structured and extensively governed by rules, the achiever is forced to conform and is prevented from being creative. The achiever, then, is significantly frustrated from acting himself. He performs poorly in these rigid situations. The worst thing you can do to the achiever is to restrict his spontaneity, block his creativity and stifle his efforts to work on things he considers significant.

Best-Matched People   The achiever gets along best with other achievers. In fact, almost all great marriages I have seen, that are cemented by deep love, true compassion, mutual understanding, clear openness, a feeling of oneness, rich renewal, and the other significant dimensions of a genuine relationship, occur between achievers. To remove your defenses so you can build an authentic, trusting friendship requires an enormous amount of self-confidence and the other skills typical of the achiever. The achiever gives to another achiever the freedom to be himself—spontaneity, openness, challenge, creativity and genuineness.

Worst-Matched People   The achiever gets along worst with the commander, for the commander violates his need for self-reliance, spontaneity, and creativity. These frustrations cause much conflict between the achiever and the commander.

General Consequences of the Achiever's Leadership Style

In mixed types of situations, achievers produce the following general results.

Efficiency   The achiever is above average in his orderliness. Although he does not attain nearly the degree of systematization the commander does, the achiever is typically as efficient as the situation demands. He keeps his goals clearly in mind, seldom strays away from the major issues, and does not become preoccupied with efficiency if it hampers effectiveness.

Morale   The morale of the achiever's subordinates is typically high. Because they are able to put themselves into their work and make significant contributions to the results, the members of his organization become significantly committed to their jobs and to their achiever-leader.

Personal Growth   The achiever urges his subordinates to take on as much responsibility as they can handle effectively. Thus, he establishes a climate where training, experience, development, questioning, and exploration are highly valued and rewarded. These factors create striking personal growth in the achiever's subordinates. Witness lies in the frequent raids other managers make on his department to hire away his people.

Organizational Growth   The achiever-leader motivates his subordinates to scan their environment, study the changes and adapt to the significant demands upon them. Since they are not afraid of the unknown, they do not ignore it, but enjoy dealing with it. His organization, then, is vital, lively, and always searching for better ways to reach its objectives.

Overall Effectiveness   The achiever-leader generally produces the most effective results of all the six types of leaders. Whenever I have asked managers to describe the best leader they have ever known personally, thousands have overwhelmingly selected the achiever. The achiever aims toward significant goals, creates genuine motivation in his subordinates to work together to attain them, initiates creative solutions to difficult problems, and faces setbacks with maturity and confidence. Furthermore, he evaluates his results continually, so he keeps his work team on course in reaching their objectives.

How Do You Best Get Along With the Achiever-Leader?

As his Superior   The best way to manage the achiever is to behave like one yourself. Be direct, honest, and real. Tell him your ideas and ask him for his. Listen carefully, react openly, and do not be afraid to challenge his thoughts. Make sure you determine which goals he thinks are meaningful, so that you can direct his behavior toward them; otherwise, he will not devote his talents to the goals. Make sure the goals you have him work on are challenging and varied. After you come to an agreement with the achiever about what he should work on, leave him alone so he can rely on his own talents to reach the objectives.

As his Subordinate   The way to work most effectively under the achiever is, again, to be an achiever. Behave as described above for his superior, and you will be highly rewarded by the achiever. Gain his agreement about what you should do, then do it without asking questions about details or seeking direction.

As his Peer Again, the most successful way to relate well with the achiever is to behave like an achiever. By doing this, you will allow him to act himself; thus, he will like you and cooperate with you.

How To be More of an Achiever

If you are an achiever and do not want to change to become one of the other five types, but desire to improve and grow toward higher levels of excellence as an achiever, you should practice:
1. Understanding your own motivations,
2. Being more self-reliant,
3. Being more spontaneous and natural,
4. Doing more of those things you believe,
5. Exploring the unknown, seeking new experiences,
6. Sharpening your perception of reality,
7. Developing close, genuine relationships, and
8. Being realistic about your goals and ideas.

By following these strategies you can enrich your life even more completely, and you can reach higher levels of fulfillment and effectiveness.

SUMMARY

Try to summarize the key concepts dealing with the achiever-leader now.

1. What are the major aspects of the achiever's leadership style?

2. In which situations does he fit best?

3. What are the general consequences of his leadership practices?

4. How do you best get along with the achiever?

5. How can the achiever change?

CHAPTER 15

Psychological Health and Effectiveness

Is There One Best Style?

In the preceding chapters, I have stressed that each of the six personality types is most effective in a best-fit-adjustment or properly matching environmental situation. Nevertheless, one question remains to be answered. "Is there one style of leadership that is generally the best?"

My experience leads me to believe that the answer is "yes." If I had to select one style to try to become, which in fact I have done, that is most effective generally for a variety of types of situations, there is no question in my mind that it is the achiever. In my research, I have asked over 3,000 individuals to select the most effective, the very best leader or manager they have ever known personally and write a detailed description of the person— examples of his behavior that indicate each of his key characteristics. Overwhelmingly, most (85%) have described achievers as the most overall effective leaders.

Similarly, I have asked them to select and describe the worst leader, the least effective person, they have known. Avoiders were selected most frequently as the worst managers. Attackers and pleasers followed respectively.

Each type of leader is effective in his best-fit-adjustment, but my research suggests that generally the achiever excels over most situations.

There are two major reasons why achievers are generally most effective. First, they are more genuinely adaptable. They adjust more easily to different environmental demands than the other five types. Second, at each higher level of administration within organizations, the environmental situation becomes more changing, unpredictable, and complex. This type of situation is most complementary to an achiever's needs. Thus, he functions most effectively in key positions. Furthermore, in top positions, the consequences of his behavior are most significant. His influence is felt by more people, more intensely, and for longer periods of time.

People are drawn to achievers, they inspire trust and health in others, and they bring out people's better qualities of humaneness and creativity. Achievers produce relatively positive results in areas that range from painting, carpentry, and plumbing, to marriage and raising children, to therapy, business management, medicine, or teaching. Whatever their calling, they do it well not because of prestige, friendship, power, fear, or aggression, but because of the sheer joy of doing what they like to do. The intrinsic pleasure of "following their gut" motivates them to act. Their actions are effective because of their style of approaching their work.

My research has indicated another interesting, albeit tentative finding along these lines. In studying new and thus small enterprises that have succeeded, two styles of leadership often combine to be the most effective. An achiever (or performer) generally provides the creative, risk-taking personnel and outside services for the firm, while a commander runs the detailed implementation, operations, bookkeeping, and productive efforts.[1] Without either of these functions, especially for new enterprises, an organization suffers. If creative, moderately risky decisions are not made, the organization cannot meet competition. If systematic information, records, and procedures are not maintained, the organization loses direction and efficiency.

If one person has a dominant need to achieve and a secondary need to command or vice versa, he can fulfill both functions for the new organization. Most often, however, two people serve these roles since these personality styles are only moderately similar.

For large organizations, a combination of three personality and

---

1. When an individual has a combination of the need to perform and the need to command he typically becomes an aggressive entrepreneur in whatever field of work he engages.

leadership styles seems to be the most effective. When a commander is in charge of the technical, production and detailed administrative functions; when a performer directs the sales and promotion activities; and when an achiever runs the human dimensions and oversees the commander and performer, my research suggests that maximum long-run effectiveness is reached.

Effectiveness and Health

A thrilling observation for me has been to discover that those individuals who are generally the most productive and creative, the achievers, are also the most psychologically healthy.

I have found achievers to be exhilarated with their lives and motivated to make themselves more fulfilled, authentic, and meaningful. They are seldom overly tense. They sleep peacefully and relaxation comes naturally for them. They are in a continual process of being, living, and becoming what they are able to become. They let their lives unfold along the paths of their unique abilities, interests, and needs, for they become what their potentials will allow. Living for them is a process of fulfilling what is inside them, not what others expect or demand of them. They are contented, involved, and active in pursuing those things that interest them.

By no means are they perfect. There are no such human beings. Anger, frustration, stubbornness, pride, nervousness, depression, fear, rejection, and loneliness all cross their paths; however, they usually flow more naturally from the situations in which they are involved and last a shorter time than for the other five types.

I believe, then, that if you want a model of life to aim toward, the achiever personality is the most effective and healthy. By no means are nonachievers completely miserable and ineffective. But compared with achievers, I believe they are less fulfilled and productive.

What if everyone became achievers? Wouldn't we all be the same and thus boring? Not at all. The achiever personality refers to the style of living, not the content. We could have achievers who were Catholics or atheists. They could be carpenters, businessmen, artists, and mechanics. The sameness that would exist would center on their all being relatively honest, spontaneous, genuine, curious, experimental, creative, open, etc. I can readily accept this commonness with others, for it would allow much more individuality than without it.

Psychological Health and Best-Fit-Adjustment

The achiever has effectiveness and psychological health then, and this is what I believe to be the ideal state for human beings. There is, however, a second state of being which many people confuse with health and effectiveness, yet which does not approach either of these goals. This is what I have called *best-fit-situation* in the preceding chapters. Best-fit situation or best-fit-adjustment exists when an individual gets into the properly matching type of organizational system, situation or environment for *his particular personality needs*. When a pleaser, for example, gets a job in an organization that rewards him for behaving as a pleaser, when he marries another pleaser, joins groups and chooses friends who reinforce and accept his "pleasing behavior," he is the most adjusted and the most effective, *given* his particular personality type. He has best-fit-adjustment. He has reached a homeostasis point.

Even though he might have best-fit-adjustment, however, he still is far from reaching his human potential for psychological health. If he were a pleaser, for example, he still would lack confidence and be anxious, worried, guilty, wishy-washy, ashamed of his feelings and beliefs, and lacking in self-reliance. Many people assume that, if you reach your best-fit-adjustment, you are fully actualized and healthy. I do not think this is true.

Interestingly, the great majority of people seek and attain best-fit-adjustment because (1) it satisfies their immediate personality needs and (2) changing from one personality type to another takes great courage, knowledge, effort, turmoil, and time. It is not easy to make ourselves do things which are painful, even though in the long run, we would be happier for it. This is a difficult decision for all of us to make.

My wish is that we could make psychological health and effectiveness our goal so that mankind could enjoy the true pleasures of living for which we have such great potential. In our present state of existence, in my judgement, the great majority of us are far from healthy and effective. There are many sunsets to see, but our eyes are unable to see them. There are many treasures to build, but our hands cannot create them.

Weak Instincts

Abraham Maslow has persuaded me by his observation that the dimensions of psychological health the achievers possess are basic biogenetic needs—weak instincts—of human beings.

He supports his contention by six, somewhat overlapping, arguments:

1. Patients in turmoil who come to therapists for help suffer from a lack of these achiever traits.

2. When therapists allow sick people to seek their own answers and solutions, they prefer to move toward these characteristics of psychological health.

3. Those who have survived the impact of their culture and are defined by clinical evidence as the most healthy and happy people display these dimensions.

4. When people express their true life preferences, most desire the traits we have given of psychological health.

5. When these needs and capacities are frustrated, people become tense, nervous, easily upset, dissatisfied.

6. When these needs are gratified, health is fostered.[2]

I was quite shocked when I read Maslow's observations because I had been such a strong believer in the environmental determinants of behavior. To find that in my clinical work and consulting experience I had been assuming for years the same things as Maslow— that man needs an environment that supports his basic push (his weak instincts) towards self-actualization—was a startling surprise. The more I thought about it, the more I realized that most other therapists, and organizational and community developers were making the same assumptions. Although the methods differ greatly, the goals are quite the same—help mankind become self-confident,

---

2. Interestingly, Maslow also notes that the animal most similar to the human, although still quite different, is the ape, who is quite cooperative, peaceful, and friendly. Many erroneous conclusions about humans are often made by comparing man to lower animals that are far different from us. (Maslow, p. 77).

trusting, honest, open, natural, spontaneous, genuine, self-reliant, in essence, more healthy, by creating appropriate environments and trying to change individual behavior. Our weak instincts can be readily undone by our cultural experiences. Therefore, make sure these experiences are positive.

Consequences of Sickness

I believe that a significant reason for our recent "generation gap" and social conflicts is that our society's dominant personality type has been the performer instead of the achiever. Our older generations have rewarded and worshipped performer personality types, and while possibly not actively opposing psychological health, have paid less attention to it.

Many of those who are striving to change our society, in contrast, have perceived the differences between performer life-patterns and achiever life-patterns and want to stress the achiever instead of the performer. Overreactions in the form of youth revolts, for example, certainly occurred; yet, the essence of a large segment of the youth revolt has been, "The performer who strives for the recognition primarily via wealth, is sick. The performer lifestyle does not come close to reaching the potential man possesses."

Many such youths I have talked with about these ideas relive experiences of seeing the emptiness their fathers' and mothers' existence. As one young lady rather poetically phrased it,

> My parents and their country club group try to make each other feel good by pretending to be happy and great. Their real sterility is hard to hide, though, even from kids. Maybe our eyes are still fresh enough to see phoniness instead of realness, to smell loneliness instead of roses. I just kept asking myself, "Why do I want to grow up to be like that? If that's all there is, stop the world and let me off."

Many youths, of course, are merely attackers joining the cover of a legitimate role to criticize and rebel against society. Others are avoiders who find drugs a way to hide from life. There are all types of personalities within the ranks of rebels. The major thrust of the responsible voices, however, are crying for a more meaningful existence, for more psychological health.

One reason that many of us in the main social institutions have reacted so strongly against the youth's revolts is that they hit close to home. It is difficult for us to accept challenges to our performer lifestyles when we have committed our lives to it. When our son says, ''Dad, all you do is work at a job that you really don't enjoy, just for money and prestige. That is stupid. I'm going to do something I really like, no matter whether I earn much or if it is popular. Especially, I am going to have fun in life and not be a 'workaholic' like you,'' this drives the blade into our hearts for it strikes what we have always considered our virtues. This is painful because unconsciously many of us have deep fears that our son is correct, for we have secretly asked ourselves the same questions many times.

Correspondingly, when our children say, ''So many people are miserable in their marriages, yet stay married just because of social pressures, when they have no genuine love—that is ridiculous''; they again are carving away one of our key foundations of the ''American performer way-of-life.'' When our children continue by saying ''I am going to live with whomever I fall in love, and leave if and when we fall out of love and not bother with that phony marriage ceremony,'' our performer desires for respectability are further shocked. Yet, we all know of the phenomenal number of marriages that are poor ones, that lack love in the deepest sense. So, again, our hidden impulses of what is right and wrong, our guilt about adultery, about mechanical sex are stirred from our unconscious by these naked challenges. Interestingly, I have found that over 80 percent of children between the ages of 15 to 60 dislike their parents. They do not like to be with them for more than a day or two at a time and then only for infrequent visits. Their explanations for disliking their parents are that, ''They do not accept me; I have to guard myself from acting how I really am. My parents do not really see me as a person.'' This by no means proves the children are correct, but it does highlight the communications and psychological health gap that exists in our present society.

Rollo May suggests that modern man has lost his ability *to feel, to experience meaningful love, friendships, and sexual relationships.* We have become so alienated from each other, so lonely that we fear to allow ourselves to feel or to love. Consequently, we seek large quantities of sex, measure the frequency, number of climaxes, and length of time involved rather than naturally enjoying the love and pleasures of sexual relationships. I think he captured well the issue that is gripping our world today—too much performance and not enough enjoyment of our real human potentials (May, p. 59).

What makes the challenges of our children even more threatening is that we indeed are not fulfilled to a large degree and look to children for authentic love. When they reject us, the meaning of our lives is raised before our eyes like a specter. As one older father, a lawyer from New York, asked me in a sorrowful, overwhelmingly sad voice, "I just don't understand them. I'm reading *The Greening of America*. My youngest son has his hair down to his shoulders, and he's off just living in Italy. What's wrong with him?"

The important point of this example and the consequences of sickness is that they illustrate the need for taking a careful look at (1) what types of personalities we have, (2) how healthy we are, (3) what causes us to be like we are, and (4) what the consequences of our personalities are for our lives, work, and families. Hopefully, by learning the answers to these questions, we will be able to better create an enriching society, a society we wish we could have been raised in and lived in. Hopefully, *The Achievers* is of some help in this direction.

If you have some experiences or insights you wish to share I would greatly appreciate your comments and reactions to the ideas presented here. Please contact me:

Dr. Jerry D. Bell
Bell Leadership
P.O. Box 572
Chapel Hill, NC 27514
919-967-7904 (phone)
919-967-3484 (fax)

APPENDIX

I will present here a brief review of the research methodology. A more thorough explanation of the research design and a technical presentation of my research findings will be presented in forthcoming professional publications. My purpose in this book is to share my conclusions with nonprofessional audiences first in hope that they might be of some help to our society. My apologies to my professional colleagues for not answering all their questions here. I hope to do so through professional journals.

The Sample

The conclusions presented in this book are based on data collected from approximately 3,000 individuals. A demographic breakdown of this sample appears in Table 1.

Data Collection

Information was gathered over a eight-year period from the 3,000 subjects by the following techniques:

Interviews My research assistants and I conducted personal interviews lasting between one and eight hours (averaging 2.5 hours) to attempt to assess each subject's personality characteristics.

Table 1
DEMOGRAPHIC CHARACTERISTICS OF THE SAMPLE

(N = approximately 3,000)

	% N
AGE	

AGE	% N	EDUCATION	
16-21	6	6 years or less	3
22-30	21	7-12 years	22
31-40	33	some college	15
41-50	27	college graduate	35
51-60	9	some prof. or grad.	14
61 +	4	prof. or grad. degree	11

INCOME		OCCUPATION	
$4,000-10,000	8	unskilled	2
$11,000-20,000	20	semiskilled	6
$21,000-30,000	35	skilled	10
$31,000-40,000	19	clerical	17
$41,000-50,000	10	lower-level management	21
$51,000 +	8	middle management	34
		top management	10

RELIGION		LOCATION	
Protestant	45		
Catholic	16	Northeast	22
Jewish	10	South	33
none	26	Middle West	28
other	3	West	17

INDUSTRY		SEX	
business	48	male	71
professional	20	female	29
government	15		
education	10		
unemployed	7		

Panels of Judges   Panels of individuals were asked to write detailed descriptions of their immediate superior. They were first asked to use their own judgments to formulate individually as complete and thorough an analysis of their boss as possible. Second, they were asked to compare their individual descriptions with those of the other panel members and to discuss their differences. They were urged to give specific examples of the subject's behavior for each characteristic they specified and to arrive at a consensus on their descriptions.

The person they described was their boss. The panel consisted of subordinates who all worked for the same individual, and other persons they knew well and with whom they worked closely.

These panels were then asked to describe and rank their subject(s) on the main concepts I have used to analyze the six personality and leadership types. For example, the panel was asked to compare their subject(s) with others on how much of a risk-taker he was, how genuinely self-confident he was, and so forth. Again, the panel members did this individually at first, then compared results and arrived at the best consensus possible. Also, they were required to give specific, detailed examples of the subject(s) behavior that caused them to rank their subject(s) as they did.

Finally, the panels were presented detailed descriptions of the six personality and leadership profiles and asked to rank their subjects on each dimension for the six types, and to compare and correct their individual rankings.

Each superior, who was himself a subject for review by a panel of his subordinates, was asked to assess each panel member. Similarly, the panel members were asked to rank each other.

Experiments

The third major technique for assessing the personality characteristics of the subjects was to have them participate in a series of experimental exercises, games, and situations that simulated real-life conditions. Conflict resolution, in-basket games, and teamwork experiments are examples of these experiments. Various measurements of the subjects' behavior, their self-rankings, and peer rankings were collected from these exercises.

Behavioral Measures

A variety of behavioral indicators were gathered to attempt to assess the subjects' motivational characteristics. For example, comparisons were made between the previous assessment conclusions for subjects and their promotion and salary history, job assignments, performance evaluations, goal-setting patterns, major interpersonal conflicts, sociometric patterns, job preferences, job successes, and failures and so forth.

Tests

A series of tests were developed and administered to the subjects. These consisted of paper-pencil tests and projective tests. The subjects completed these about themselves and their subordinates, peers, and boss.

Relevant Research

I should note briefly that my research suggests that McClelland, Atkinson and others, who contributed so brilliantly to the subject of motivation, combined several types of needs. For example, the following TAT story which McClelland, *et al.* score as high on need for achievement would be scored moderately high on the need to attack in my scoring system, and not high on the need for achievement.

> Wilhelm Schmitzig, age 9, turns his finely chiseled features into the sunlight of another happy day and for a moment forgets the algebra lesson he has to do. Be a doctor—be a doctor, the passion of his idealistic youth is strong in his desire to be a surgeon like his father, now dead. Porato—porato—the anesthetizing machine hums on as Walter Schmitzig performs a delicate operation on a man who was doomed to die. Eventually Wilhelm will be tossed out of school for failing algebra. He will degenerate slowly until finally his sole income will be derived from window washing. (David C. McClelland, *The Achievement Motive*, 1953, p. 360, Story 22-4)

Similarly, much research in psychology has either combined the need to avoid failure with the need for achievement in an additive fashion in analyzing data, or assumed the absence of need for achievement implies the presence of the need to avoid failure and vice versa. My research would strongly suggest both of these assumptions are inaccurate (See McClelland, 1961 and Atkinson, 1964).

The great majority of the 3,000 individuals I have studied answered these questions as follows:

1. Achievers were the overwhelming first choice, performers were second and commanders third.

3. Avoiders stood alone in claiming the worst position. Attackers and pleasers followed.

5. The person you selected is one who is most similar and compatible with your personality needs. You can see yourself in a mirror when you look at their personality type.

6. The person you selected is most similar to you in personality needs, and one with whom you can be honest. If you rated yourself as very much on the question you tend to be: 7. A commander, 8. An attacker, 9. An avoider, 10. A pleaser, 11. A performer, 12. An achiever.

BIBLIOGRAPHY

John W. Atkinson, *An Introduction to Motivation*. New York: American Book Co., 1964.

———, and Norman T. Feather, *A Theory of Achievement Motivation*. New York: John Wiley & Sons, Inc., 1966.

Gerald D. Bell, "Aspiration Levels of Lower Class, High I. Q. Males." *Social Forces* (March 1963).

Allan Bullock, *Hitler*. New York: Harper & Row, 1962.

Robert Coles, *Uprooted Children*. New York: Harper & Row, 1970.

Benjamin Franklin, *The Autobiography of Benjamin Franklin*. New York: Washington Square Press, Inc., 1966.

Erich Fromm, *Man for Himself*. New York: Holt, Rinehart and Winston, Inc., 1947.

John W. Gardner, *Excellence*. New York: Harper & Row, 1961.

Erving Goffman, *The Presentation of Self in Everyday Life*. Garden City, N. Y.: Doubleday & Co., 1959.

Thomas Harris, *I'm Okay, You're Okay*. New York: Harper & Row, 1969.

O. W. Harvey, David E. Hunt, and Harold M. Schroder, *Conceptual Systems and Personality Organization*. New York: John Wiley & Sons, Inc., 1961.

Heinz Heckhausen, *The Anatomy of Achievement Motivation*. New York: Academic Press, 1967.

Karen Horney, *Our Inner Conflicts*. New York: W. W. Norton & Co., Inc., 1945.

Ken Kesey, *One Flew over the Cuckoo's Nest*. New York: The Viking Press, 1962.

Harold Leavitt, *Managerial Psychology*. Chicago: University of Chicago Press, 1969.

Abraham H. Maslow, *Motivation and Personality*. New York: Harper & Bros., 1954, rev. ed. 1970.

Rollo May, *Love and Will*. New York: W. W. Norton & Co., Inc., 1959.

David C. McClelland, *The Achievement Motive*. New York: Appleton-Century-Crofts, Inc., 1953.

―――, *The Achieving Society*. New York: The Free Press, 1961.

Henry Miller, *Big Sur and the Orange of Hieronymus Bosch*. New York: New Directions Publishing Corp., 1957.

Carl Rogers, *On Becoming a Person*. Boston: Houghton Mifflin Co., 1961.

Milton Rokeach, *The Open and Closed Mind*. New York: Basic Books, 1960.

Stanley Schachter, *The Psychology of Affiliation*. Stanford: Stanford University Press, 1959.

Alfred P. Sloan, Jr., *My Years with General Motors*. New York: MacFadden Books, 1963.

Abraham Zaleznik, *Human Dilemmas of Leadership*. New York: Harper & Row, 1966.